CUTTING HAIR THE

VIDAL SASSOON

WAY

CUTTING HAIR THE
VIDAL SASSOON
WAY

SECOND EDITION

BUTTERWORTH
HEINEMANN

Butterworth-Heinemann Ltd
Linacre House, Jordan Hill, Oxford OX2 8DP

ℛ A member of the Reed Elsevier group

OXFORD   LONDON   BOSTON
MUNICH   NEW DELHI   SINGAPORE   SYDNEY
TOKYO   TORONTO   WELLINGTON

First published 1978
Reprinted 1981
Second edition 1984
Reprinted 1985, 1987, 1988, 1991, 1993

ISBN 0 7506 0324 0

Printed and bound in Great Britain by
BAS Printers Limited, Over Wallop, Hampshire

CONTENTS

The book is further illustrated with photographs from
the Vidal Sassoon Library

DEDICATION

I believe that the sharing of knowledge and ideas provide the most positive way to encourage innovation and creativity within our profession. This book sets out the basic principles that I have found invaluable. Some of these ideas were gifts. Others I evolved through trial and error. It is my hope that this text will serve merely as a foundation from which your own style and individuality will emerge.

'IT'S THE CUT THAT COUNTS . . .'

This startlingly simple philosophy is the basis of one of the most famous and successful hairdressing empires ever known. It is the philosophy of VIDAL SASSOON, the world's leading authority on the care and the cutting of hair.

Since Vidal Sassoon started his first salon in London, the name has became synonymous with all that is best in haircutting. Once he made his first impact on the international fashion scene, the unfailing variety, innovation, and appeal of Sassoon cuts – many of which have become classics – have never ceased to be a credit to the profession, and today the Vidal Sassoon organization is acknowledged as the major influence on hairdressing all over the world and an inspiration to hairdressers everywhere.

How did it all begin? Vidal was born in London on 17 January 1928 and his family lived for some time in the East End where Vidal, as a small boy, enjoyed roaming around Petticoat Lane, one of London's most colourful street markets. At the outbreak of war Vidal's mother, Betty, decided London was not safe for her young son and packed him off to the country where he worked in a glove factory, learning very quickly how to cut leather with an expertise that served him well later on!

But Vidal missed his family so badly that his mother agreed to his returning home in 1942. This was the time of the regular German air raids on London and Vidal got a job as a messenger boy, riding a broken-down bike through the Blitz. In his spare time he played football with his friends and at one time dreamt of making football his career. But his mother, with her usual good sense, decided that her fourteen-year-old son must learn a proper trade and apprenticed him, somewhat against his will, to 'Professor' Adolf Cohen, a well-known hairdresser in Whitechapel Road, a bustling thoroughfare in London's East End.

The apprenticeship was not easy; whatever needed doing, Vidal had to do it, from sweeping the floor to making the tea, and it was some time before he was allowed the privilege of becoming a shampoo boy. He admits he did not like hairdressing very much but he knew he had to earn his own living. So with characteristic enthusiasm and determination he made up his mind that if he had to be a hairdresser then he was going to be the *best*.

As Vidal recalls, 'Professor' Cohen was a talented and kind man and he tried to teach his newest recruit all he knew. Vidal sensed, however, that to get to the top in what was now his chosen profession he must work in the centre of London and therefore he decided to find himself a job in the more elegant West End.

He had his share of refusals but eventually he was taken on and trained for short periods by several of the leading London hairdressers of the time. He learned something from each and when he had absorbed enough, he moved on to the next. It was a hard and demanding time for a youngster but it provided Vidal with the firm foundation on which his whole future career and generous philosophy has been built.

The last stop in Vidal's run-up to independence was with Raymond whose originality, dash, and energy were revitalizing London's hairdressing scene in the early fifties.

Of Raymond, whom he still regards as one of his mentors, Vidal says, 'merely to watch him experiment and try out new techniques was an education . . . he boosted my confidence and encouraged me to think along entirely new lines'.

In his autobiography, *Sorry I Kept You Waiting, Madam*, Vidal writes of a major turning point in his career:

'Many people helped to mould me. In doing so, they brought me to the end of an era. I realised that the time had come for *me* to do some moulding! Around me I could see clothes that had a wonderful shape to them, and all because of the cutting. I wanted to see hair keeping up with fashion, maybe jumping ahead of it, leading it along a certain line, instead of lagging behind it. I wanted to shape heads as the new young fashion designers were shaping bodies. I wanted to cut hair as they cut cloth. I wanted to be in on the revolution that was simmering—but I knew that I would not rebel while I was working for other people. So, when I left Raymond, I did not look for another job. Instead I looked for a salon of my own.'

So, in 1954 Vidal opened on his own in Bond Street, Mayfair—just one small room up a steep flight of stairs. Legend now has it that Vidal was a success overnight. But, as Vidal confirms, this is far from the truth. Business for the first few years was far from easy. His ideas about hair were revolutionary and he refused to compromise. He spent those first years perfecting and polishing his techniques of cutting that were to cause a total revaluation in every major hairdressing salon round the world. Gradually word got around that there was this crazy young man in Bond Street who was trying to do something really new with hair. Actresses, top models, and one or two far-seeing journalists realised his potential and became excited and enthusiastic about the Sassoon philosophy—'It's the cut that counts'. This fresh approach to hair—combined with an irresistible, irrepressible Cockney sense of humour—often drew people to the Sassoon salon out of curiosity. But they liked what they saw, they liked their new-looking hair, and they came back for more, bringing their friends with them.

The so-called 'Swinging Sixties' which put London on the world fashion map proved to be the watershed in Vidal's professional life. In fashion, in beauty, in hair, it was all happening in London and Vidal played a major role in producing a look to match the changing lifestyle of women everywhere. Nothing would ever be the same again. In 1964 Vidal created the first, famous Five Point Geometric Cut on a young model named Grace Coddington, who is now the Fashion Editor of British *Vogue*. The photograph of this cut—which Vidal still considers his finest—went around the world and provided the cornerstone of his international success.

London's brightest fashion revolutionary, Mary Quant, was also doing her own exciting thing in a tiny room in the now famous King's Road in Chelsea. She saw Vidal shaping hair in the same sharp, simple way she cut fabric and soon she too had a Sassoon Geometric style. They became friends and ideas sparked from one to the other, neither of them ever being totally satisfied with what they did. As innovators, as creators, they did not stand still. This is still true today.

Famous fashion designers in Paris and Rome invited the young British hairdresser to create styles specially for them and in 1965 Emmanuel Ungaro, a dramatic new force in unprecedented modern design, asked Vidal to produce a style to complement his collection in Paris. The result was the Asymmetric Cut, acknowledged around the fashion world as yet another important new Sassoon concept in cutting.

In 1967 Vidal created another sensation with The Greek Goddess. It was, in his words, 'the geometric cut gone curly'. It was a basic Sassoon blunt cut, permed and dried with a heat lamp while the stylist ran his or her fingers rather than a brush or comb through the hair.

By this time Vidal's reputation was truly international and by 1965 he had taken another major plunge, opening his first salon in New York. A perfectionist, as always, Vidal realised that his arrival in America had to be an EVENT—and it certainly was. The party was acknowledged as a sensation: sausages and mash, mugs of beer, and stunning model girls with haircuts the like of which had never been seen in New York. So many people came, both invited and uninvited, that the party spilled out into the street. Vidal had arrived in grand style and the next day the newspapers were hailing him as a dazzling new star in the American fashion firmament.

Immediately the name Vidal Sassoon became the password to style and anyone who wanted to be considered as part of the New York scene simply *had* to have a cut by the Master. Other Sassoon salons followed – Chicago, Los Angeles, San Francisco and now there is a chain of salons and schools in the United States, Canada, Germany and, of course, England.

So the boy from London had 'made it' and, just as he had done at home, he had revolutionized the craft of haircutting in the New World.

Success brought nationwide fame; he appeared on the most popular TV shows and hosted, along with his No. 1 Creative Director, Christopher Brooker, huge cutting demonstrations across the country. Leading newspapers and magazines featured the Sassoon lifestyle.

American women who loved the new freedom movement in hair soon 'adopted' Vidal as an honorary citizen. He was talented, he worked hard, he had a tremendous sense of humour, and a deep social conscience. There had never been anyone even remotely like him on the American hairdressing scene before and the entire profession there, as elsewhere, benefited greatly from his influence. What Vidal had done was to free women from the elaborate 'dressing' of hair. The world had changed, so had women's lives and they no longer wanted to spend hours every week (and some even every day) sitting in rollers under a hot dryer.

They wanted hair to complement their new more mobile lives—rushing out in the morning to go to work or take the children to school—and then feeling confident enough to go out in the evening without having to worry about having their hair 'done'. So the Sassoon slogan 'It's the cut that counts' became the order of the day as women found that if they had a good cut once a month they could easily look after their own hair in the intervening weeks. *But* and this is an important 'but', in the Sassoon philosophy, a good cut cannot succeed with hair in bad condition. Smoke-filled rooms, air pollution, normal wear and tear, chemical treatments and, above all, too much summer sun take their toll and hair must be 'fed' regularly to keep it in tip-top condition.

To encourage women everywhere to regard their hair as a precious asset requiring specialized, gentle treatment, an extensive range of Sassoon Hair Care products for both consumer and trade have been developed. These products, sold internationally through very many professional hair salons and retail trade outlets are revolutionizing thinking everywhere about the right and wrong way to keep hair clean and healthy. In today's environment it is now recognized that hair, like skin, needs a cleanse, tone, and condition regime and this is the basis of the Sassoon philosophy.

However, if hair-care is No. 1 priority in Sassoon thinking, then there is one other contender for top place. In a world where specialized knowledge is closely guarded the Vidal Sassoon organization is acknowledged as unique. It believes now, as it has always done, that its talented and creative team have a responsibility to hairdressers of the future which goes far beyond its own staff.

To further teaching and to raise the standards of the entire profession, schools and academies have been opened in the UK, and the United States.

The purpose of the Sassoon educational programme is two-fold. The first is to train staff for the Sassoon salons. At the end of the training period there is a stiff test and no one is allowed on to any salon floor until he or she is qualified. The second is to offer courses to experienced hairdressers from all over the world to learn the specialized Sassoon techniques. Thousands of hairdressers – from beginners to experts – enrol every year to perfect their techniques and learn from the Sassoon Creative team what ideas are in the air. Because Vidal Sassoon took the conscious decision to pass on the secrets of his expertise, it is now possible for a fashion-conscious woman to get Sassoon-style haircutting virtually anywhere in the world.

Men are not neglected by the Team and Vidal Sassoon Barber Shops are as successful as the ladies' salons. These Barber Shops are carefully designed with men in mind, even if some of the clients do want a permanent wave.

The international headquarters of the Vidal Sassoon Group of companies is now based in Los Angeles. As Chairman of his fast-growing 'empire', Vidal rarely has the opportunity today to get behind the chair. But his eagle eye is constantly on everything that goes on. With his team of international stylists headed by Christopher Brooker, International Creative Director and Anne Humphreys, International Head of Colour and Technical Research, he travels all over the world giving demonstrations, promoting the company and its products and, of course, regularly visiting the salons and schools.

He is tireless in striving to maintain the highest possible standards and wherever he goes he gives confidence and inspiration to each and every member of his vast staff. One reason why he is able to do all this is because his enthusiasm never wanes and because he keeps extremely fit. His regime is strict: plenty of exercise (swimming and jogging), fresh air (he walks whenever possible) and healthy eating. His diet is based on fresh fruit and vegetables, salads, wholewheat bread, and honey which, in his own words, 'boosts the energy level'.

To spread the good word about the good life, Vidal and former wife Beverly wrote a book entitled *A Year of Beauty and Health* which was published in 1976 in North America, the United Kingdom and Australia. It stayed on the best-seller lists in America for more than six months and is now available in a paperback edition.

So now you know what Vidal Sassoon is all about . . . read, mark, and learn from the rest of the book and if you want to make your hair your business it should help you on your way. Everything that follows is dedicated to hairdressers everywhere . . . to those who are inexperienced but interested as well as those who are experienced but willing to learn more.

And even to those who think they know it all already!

THE PSYCHOLOGY OF HAIRCUTTING
How to Make a Perfect Match
between Client and Cut

WHEN THE HAIR IS DRY

There are many factors to be taken into consideration when choosing the right haircut for your client. The amount of time you spend with her BEFORE cutting is every bit as important as the time you actually work with your scissors.

Take a long, careful look at your client's total appearance as she comes into the salon. Direct your professional eye away from the style and condition of her hair for those first few moments. Concentrate instead on *her*, her height, her build. These will give you an indication of the length and cut she could and should wear. THE CUT MUST ALWAYS BE IN PROPORTION TO THE SIZE AND SHAPE OF THE BODY. For example, a tall, slim woman with a short crop will look even taller and thinner, and a short, plump woman will not look her best with hair way past her shoulders.

Study the way she dresses and how fashion-conscious she is. What you see should tell you how adventurous to be with the cut you are about to do.

How old is she? Should her age influence what you do? Hair, in fact, can be cut to almost any length at any age and look good. It is bone structure and hair texture, not age, that should determine cut and style throughout a woman's life. What *should* change is the degree of softness and movement in the cut. An older woman will find that a softer edge, less geometry and more waves or curls or gentle movement will be more becoming.

Find out as much as possible about your client's personality during that vital initial chat. Personality is not always easy to judge on a first meeting, and there are no rules for making observations or coming to conclusions. It will be a technique you learn and improve upon as you go along. DO NOT BE AFRAID TO ASK QUESTIONS! Your client's lifestyle is of the utmost importance so try to find out, for example, if she has a lot of leisure time or whether her schedule is hectic. Does she lead an outdoor or indoor life? And what about the type of community in which she lives? Try to gauge what she expects from a haircut, and how well she would manage it between visits to the salon.

All these factors determine the kind of cut you should give her, not only to make her look her best but to ensure that she feels happy and confident with the result. Give her the wrong cut and no matter how expertly it has been done, she will be self-conscious and uncomfortable.

Remember, your client when she leaves your hands and your salon takes your reputation with her. And everyone in the world outside who sees and appreciates your work *could* become a future client.

WHEN THE HAIR IS WET

It is essential that hair should be thoroughly shampooed and conditioned before cutting and you should approach your cut when the hair is wet.

There are a number of reasons for this:

1. You have better control over the hair in its wet state, because it will not slip through your fingers or away from the scissors.

2. You will be able to see the shape of the head quite plainly and, as you cut, the shape will emerge more clearly.
3. The curl you may have thought natural when the hair was dry might have been achieved with rollers.
4. A smooth blow-dry may have been hiding a profusion of natural curls or waves. With wet hair you will be able to see the natural movements and capitalize on them.
5. A simple point, but an important one—IT IS MUCH MORE HYGIENIC TO DEAL WITH CLEAN HAIR!
When the hair is wet, you will be able to observe the natural growth pattern of the hairline, particularly in the nape. For example, if the nape hair grows upward and stands out, a flat-naped cut will not work. NEVER FORCE THE HAIR AGAINST ITS GROWTH. Whatever peculiarities the hairline may have and whatever difficulties this may present, it will be a major factor in the design of your cut and could well form the positive basis for it.

Hair always moves from a natural point on the crown. Your very first move should be to find this point. When working from the crown, a parting should always start from or end at this point. You can place the parting anywhere as long as the natural growth pattern of the hair is observed and followed. This pattern should be followed throughout the whole cut, so that the finished result will complement the shape of the head.

Hair is the only substance on the human body which can be moulded and shaped into different forms. So use the skull as your basic foundation and the hair as your 'material' when shaping these forms.

PROPORTIONS

When you look at a face, you see its individual features—those which make every person different. What is not obvious at first is that all human faces have a certain common symmetry. Try these simple tests and see for yourself.

1. If you measure from the top of the head to the chin, the eyes will always be at the middle point.
2. A measurement from pupil to pupil of each eye will be equal to measurement from the bridge of the nose to its tip.
3. The mouth will always be a quarter of the way up the total measurement of the face to the chin.
4. The length of the ears is equal to the length of the nose, and both are on the same level.

These proportions are used by artists when painting or drawing the human face. Use them as a guideline for your cut.

If you are aware of all the factors mentioned in this section, you will achieve greater precision and accuracy in your cutting technique.

BONE STRUCTURE

The study of bone structure should be an important part of any haircutter's training. When you look at a face and see its features, you should also look beyond these to the basic bone structure, which is the foundation of the shape. There are no *rules* for cutting to bone structure because a haircut must, above all, be individual, but there are important factors of which every haircutter must be aware. In general, the female skull is usually smaller than the male and the external occipital protuberance and the curved lines are less defined. Although in most cases the differences in bone formation between the male and female can easily be seen, there are female skulls which do have male characteristics and here very severe haircuts should be avoided.

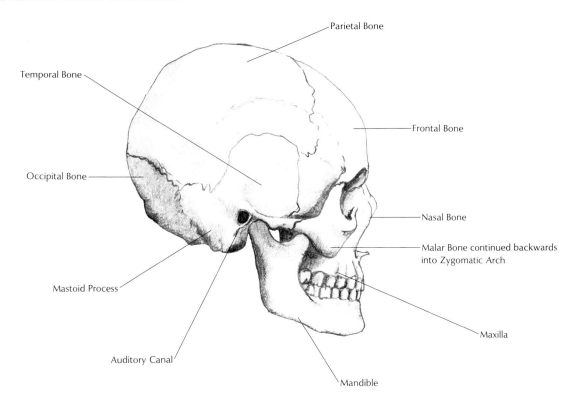

How the outline of the head is determined by the skull.

HAIR CARE AND CONDITIONING

The main theme of this book is how to achieve the excellence in haircutting which is synonymous with the name Vidal Sassoon. However, it would be incomplete without mentioning conditioning and hair care. The secret of beautiful hair relies as much upon conditioning as it does upon superb cutting. If the hair is in top condition, the finished result will look better and last longer. Cuts will shine and swing, curls will be bubbly and free from frizz.

The five stages of hair care:

1. **Cleanse and Prepare**

   Healthy, shining hair starts with the correct shampoo, used in a proper manner. There are three vital things to remember:

   (a) The shampoo you use should be acid-balanced which leaves the scalp and hair in the required slightly acid state. Today's modern shampoos employ various conditioning and moisturizing agents to compensate for the deep cleansing action of the shampoo itself. Pro-vitamin B-5 and micronized proteins are examples of excellent materials which penetrate into and act upon the hair giving it additional body and strength.

   (b) Shampoo should be used in small quantities, with sufficient activity to cleanse the hair. If, during the first application there are lasting stable suds, they demonstrate that all waxes, oils, and grime have been totally emulsified and there is still additional activity in the shampoo, and one application is sufficient. Only if the suds dissipate rapidly is a second shampoo necessary.

   (c) All traces of shampoo must be rinsed away very thoroughly. Residual shampoo is highly undesirable and many 'dandruff' complaints are the result of insufficient rinsing and the resulting residual activity on the scalp which creates dryness.

2. **Conditioners**

   The list of damaging agents affecting the hair includes chemical processing, illness, sun, improper or over-frequent blow-drying, heat, water and, of course, the increasing age of the hair itself as it grows.

   Liquid Hydrolyzed Protein is the finest known reconditioner of damaged hair, both internally and externally. A small amount of this substance when applied, actually becames a part of the hair itself! Properly acidified (pH 6.0), a liquid protein conditioner not only strengthens the hair shaft, but smooths the cuticle of the hair, restoring lustre and sheen. In effect, it fills in the damaged areas of the hair shaft. After conditioning, all excess material not absorbed should be thoroughly rinsed away. No client will thank you for leaving hair in a sticky, lack-lustre condition.

3. **Texturizing**

   Modern chemistry today provides a means of 'texturizing' hair through the use of a finishing rinse. A proper finishing rinse removes all tangles from the hair shaft and will add pro-vitamin B-5 in sufficient amounts to give extra body to the hair. Rough, wiry hair will remain in the desired softened condition if *cool* water is used to rinse off any excess. Fine and/or oily hair will maintain the additional body but will fluff if warm to hot water is used. Upon completion of the rinse, the acidification and moisturizer will leave the hair with the required sheen.

4. **Seal and Protect**

    Sealing and protection can be given to the hair shaft with periodical use of the Sassoon Protein Pac Treatments. Micronized proteins are absorbed by the hair and special protective moisturizers 'plate' the hair, creating super sheen plus protection against the harsh action of blow-dryers, hot irons, etc. Treatments are generally used when hair is in a severely damaged condition with dry and frizzy ends and/or breakage. Two or three treatments are usually necessary to restore the hair to good condition and from time to time these should be carried out professionally in the salon. It is important for your client to understand that one treatment cannot work miracles. As with health and diet, a regime of continuous care is needed to achieve and maintain the desired results. Your reward and your client's reward will be beautiful and healthy hair to complement the creative stylist's haircut.

5. **Home Hair Care**

    It is very important that the client understands that a home hair-care maintenance programme be followed to keep the hair in its luxurious condition once the professional has accomplished the reconditioning. The same super quality shampoo should be used in conjunction with remoisturizing creme treatments. A monthly conditioning regime should become part of your client's own programme to *maintain* sheen, flexibility, and hair health.

    One final thought:

    A regular haircut will remove dead, split ends and the untidy effect of irregular growth. It will emphasize the beautiful, free-swinging movement of hair which will be as thick at the ends as it is at the roots.

HANDY HINTS FOR HAIRCUTTERS
From the Vidal Sassoon Creative Team

All good stylists, however rigorously they have been trained in a particular method of cutting, should have a very open and total individual approach to their craft. It is the so-called little things that make the difference between a good haircutter and a great one.

We at Vidal Sassoon, encouraged by Christopher Brooker, believe that we can learn a great deal from each other. An exchange of ideas and collaboration inside a salon as well as competition from outside give a tremendous stimulus to any cutter and is vital to the progress of our craft. Try to treat each day and every head of hair as a new experience and try to build up a memory bank of all the ideas that develop and the hints that you pick up.

Here are just a few useful tips that the Vidal Sassoon Creative Team would like to share with you:

1. When you have finished cutting a bob, ask your client to stand up. You can then see the perfection of the line clearly from underneath. This procedure can also be carried out *while* cutting.

2. An excellent way of softening fringes and outline shapes is by 'pointing'. With the very point of the scissors, just 'skim' the hair. By using this method you will cut only the minimum and avoid hard lines.

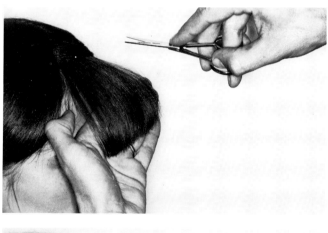

3. A mirror can be a cutter's second-best friend!
   (a) Back mirrors have an infinite number of uses. On a graduated cut, check the graduation by placing the mirror under the hairline. Any error will show clearly in the reflection. Place the mirror above your client's head to check evenness of the volume all over.
   (b) If the salon in which you work has mirrors on all walls, make full use of them by glancing in the mirror to your left or right, thus checking the total look from all sides without having to walk around your client to do so.
   (c) An easy way to check that two sides of a cut are even is to stand either directly behind your client, or facing her, and place a back-mirror at each side of her head. You will then be able to see both sides at the same time.
4. Stand away from your client occasionally as you cut, and again when you finish. Looked at from a distance, the total haircut becomes smaller, so the eye can take in more at a glance and can see any discord or disproportion more easily.
5. A good tip for checking weight in graduation is to brush the hair in the opposite direction from which it has been cut and then let it fall free. Imperfections in the graduation will be clearly seen.
6. For a final check after cutting a crop or an 'Afro' style, stand at your client's side and slowly tilt her head away from you and then back, keeping your eyes firmly fixed on the outline. Repeat this procedure standing *behind* the client. Whichever way the head is turned, the outline should remain the same.
7. Always be careful not to over-dry the hair when using a hand-dryer. Not only is this bad for the hair, but it will cause static and the hair will become difficult to manage.
8. Light tends to reflect from within curls thus making it difficult to concentrate on the actual shape of the cut. Try half-closing your eyes. You will find that your eyelashes block out light reflections and the silhouette becomes clear.
9. Always keep a water-spray close at hand, especially when cutting curly hair. When the cut is finished a fine spray of water will bring the curls back to the natural shape.
10. A fool-proof method of checking short and curly or wavy cuts is to brush all the hair forward from the nape, then backwards from the forehead, then to each side. The shape should remain constant.
11. It is a common fallacy that the cut before a perm need not be absolutely perfect because any error will be hidden by the curls. This is not so! The cut has to be exact or the hair shape will be distorted.
12. Make a thorough inspection of the features of your client's head. For example, feel the shape of the skull for any irregularities, look at ear protrusion, the density of the hair, any changes in texture, and any scars or birthmarks on the scalp. Make allowances for them.
13. Do not fight hairlines. Work *with* them!
14. Before cutting hair short, check carefully for double or triple crowns. You will have to make allowances and adjustments for these when cutting.
15. Try to keep your client's neck and shoulders as free from clothing as possible while you are cutting. You will then be able to see the overall shape from crown to nape more clearly.
16. The section you are cutting should always be thin enough for you to see the previous one through it so that you always have a guide from which to work.
17. When forming a shape, it helps to have a piece of white card handy. Particularly with dark hair, the shape will show up clearly if you place the card behind and then in front of the head.

THE TOOLS OF THE TRADE

It is vital to your skill and professionalism that your equipment is of the highest quality. If it is not, it will let you down badly.
Here is a list of the major items of equipment you will need and others you may find useful.

Scissors
Scissor length is very important. More control is achieved by using a short blade (4–4 ½ inches) when cutting free-hand—for example on fringes and graduation. For 'Afro' hair, longer scissors (5–5 ½ inches) are advisable because it is easier to envisage the shape you are cutting when the hand is further away from the hair. You are also less likely to 'dent' the hair shape by knocking it with your cutting hand. Longer scissors are also used for cutting very long hair.
KEEP SCISSORS REALLY SHARP AT ALL TIMES and spare no expense in maintaining them.

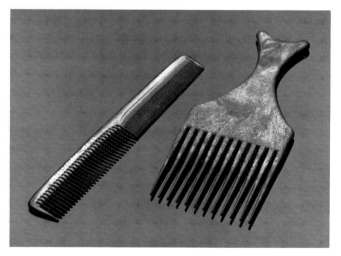

Combs
Cheap metal and plastic combs with rough edges between the teeth tear and split the hair. Vidal Sassoon combs are made of a very hard rubber and, with their smoothness and flexibility, do not harm the hair in any way. When using a scissor-over-comb method of cutting you will get better results with a tapered comb.

'Afro' Comb
The teeth on these combs are particularly well-spaced and are used on 'Afro' and very curly hair. They lift the hair out to its maximum volume without pulling, tugging or straightening. This comb is absolutely essential when dealing with 'Afro' hair and is also useful for the final touches to a curly cut.

Brushes

Vidal Sassoon brushes have nylon bristles with rounded ends set into a flexible rubber pad, thus preventing damage to the hair and providing a gentle curve to encourage natural movement when blow-drying. They are very hygienic as they can easily be taken apart for washing. Use a small brush when drying short layers and progress to a large brush as the layers get longer.

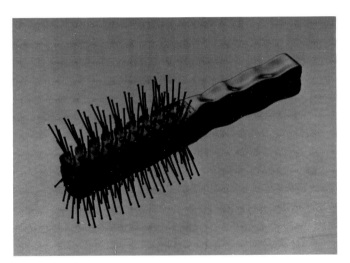

Vent Brush

A vent brush is useful when working on naturally curly hair.

Hair-dryer

A strong, good quality hand-held dryer is essential for everyday use in the salon. The Vidal Sassoon hair-dryer is extremely durable and has a number of safety features.

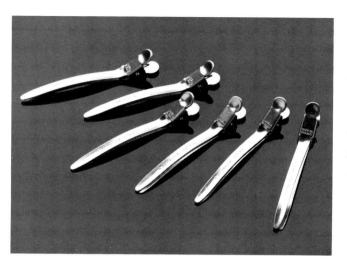

Sectioning Clips

After making a clean section it is important that the hair is combed thoroughly from the roots to the ends before cutting. If each strand of hair is not combed through, the line that you cut will be uneven when the hair falls free. To ensure that you comb the hair correctly, use one or more sectioning clips to secure the rest of the hair away from the section that you are combing.

Tongs

Tongs are very useful for giving a final touch to a side-brushed fringe, or a sleek bob. They are sometimes used on short layered cuts when extra volume is needed.

Neck Brush

Use a neck brush to remove tiny shavings of hair from your client's neck and face. A towel or tissue will only rub the hair into the skin.

Heat Lamp

A heat lamp is perfect for drying curly hair. Unlike a hair-dryer, it does not blow the curls into an uneven shape because it produces only gentle radiant heat. Heat lamps are not *essential* to the finish of a curly cut but, as they speed the drying process, they can add to the efficiency of a salon and also help the client who is in a hurry.

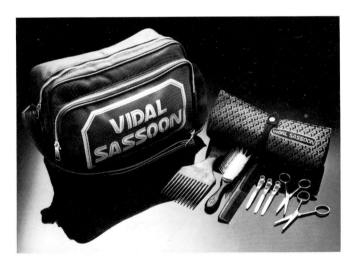

Kit Holder

This will keep your equipment clean and tidy, and you will look more professional if you do not have to dig around in the bottom of a plastic bag!

Shoulder Bag

A convenient and attractive bag in which to carry your kit holder, hair-dryer, and any spare equipment.

ALL EQUIPMENT SHOULD BE KEPT SCRUPULOUSLY CLEAN AT ALL TIMES. *COMBS IN PARTICULAR SHOULD BE WASHED AND PLACED IN A BOWL OF ANTISEPTIC AFTER EVERY CLIENT.*

Cut 1

GRADUATED BOB

Maxine is a student of fashion design. She wanted an eye-catching haircut to go with her fashionable clothes because she is constantly meeting people who will be able to help her in her future career. Her hair has a soft texture but it is also heavy, and her hairline is neat and flat—an essential quality for this haircut. The shape we cut brings out her small, neat features.

TOOLS REQUIRED:
Small scissors, small brush, large brush, comb, and hand-dryer.

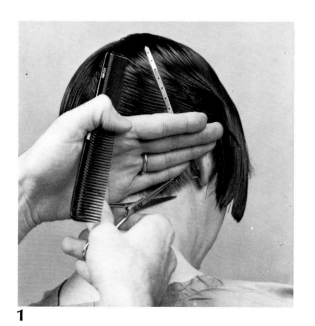

1

FIG. 1
After shampooing, part the hair in the centre from crown to nape. Section off at a downwards 45° angle towards the right ear. Comb down evenly and cut in the base line.

2

FIGS. 2, 3, 4, 5, 6, 7, 8, 9, 10, 11
Hold the section at the same angle as the line of the haircut, i.e. from the base of the occipital bone to the point of the chin.
Lift the hair out approximately 45° from the head and slightly to the centre. Cut parallel to the angle of the section (Figs. 2 & 3).
The second section (Figs. 4, 5, 6) is cut into shape using the first section as a guide for length, allowing for slight graduation.
Continue, working in sections, lifting the hair and keeping the 45° angle. Use each previously-cut section as a guideline.
ALWAYS KEEP SECTIONS CLEAN AND EVEN.

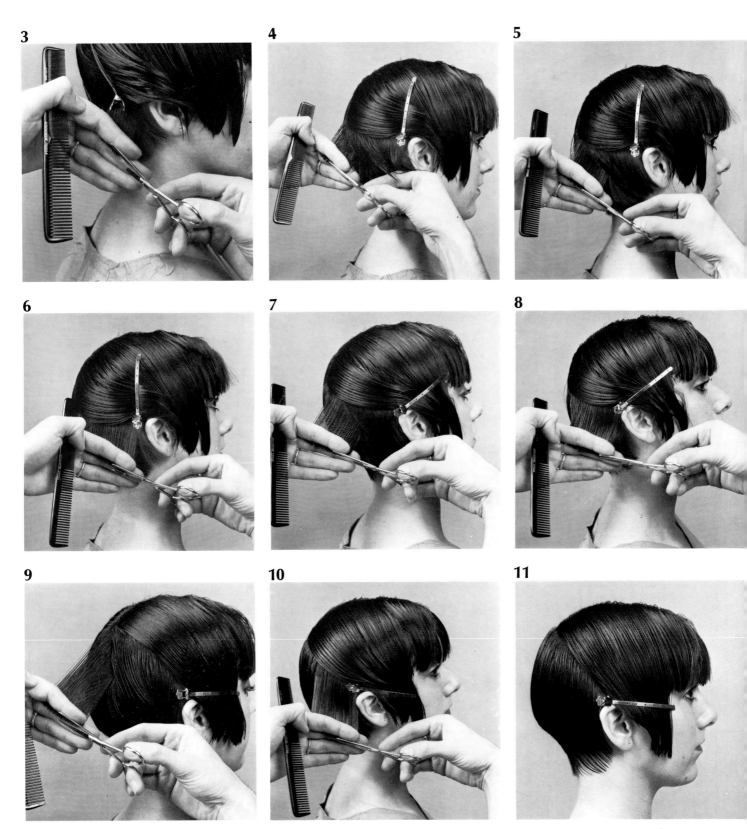

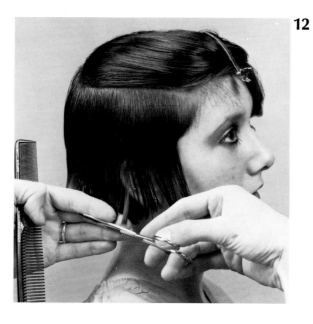

12

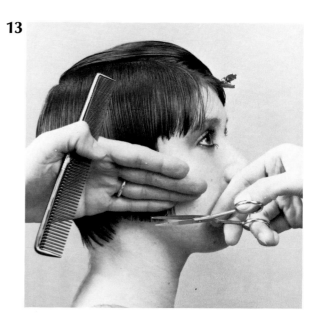

13

FIGS. 12, 13, 14, 15, 16

Part from crown to temple.

Use a small section of the back as a guide to continue the line through the side.

The hair in front of the ear is held down on the skin and cut.

CAUTION: ALLOW FOR EAR PROTRUSION. DO NOT CUT TOO SHORT!

Continue in exactly the same way.

14

15

GRADUATED BOB · 28

16

FIG. 17
Halfway
Return to the centre parting at the back. Using the line and length of the right side as a guide, continue the base-line into the left side.

17

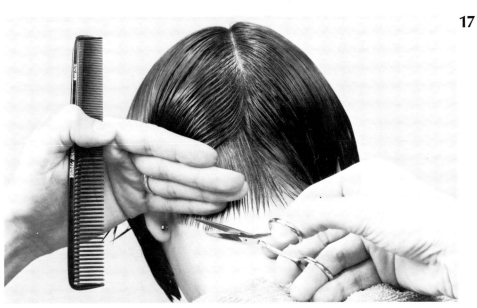

18

21

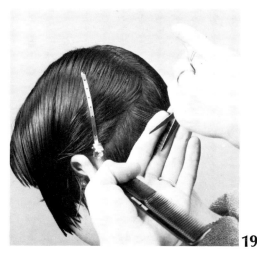

19

22

20

FIGS. 18, 19, 20, 21, 22
Graduate left-hand-side using 45°
angles as before, holding hair down
and to the centre.

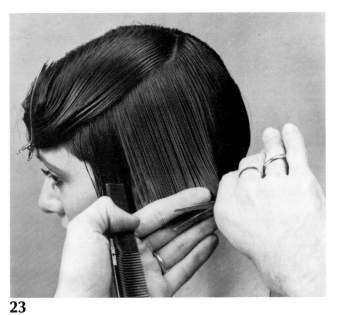

23

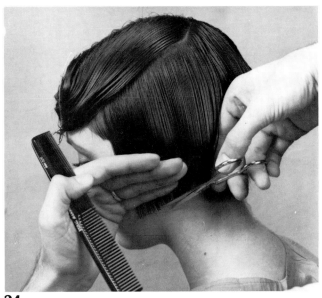

24

FIGS. 23, 24, 25, 26
Again use a small section of the back as a guide to continue the line through the side.
CAUTION: DO NOT FORGET TO ALLOW FOR EAR!

25

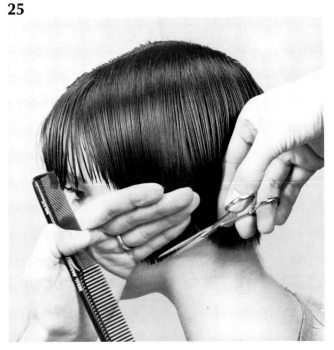

26

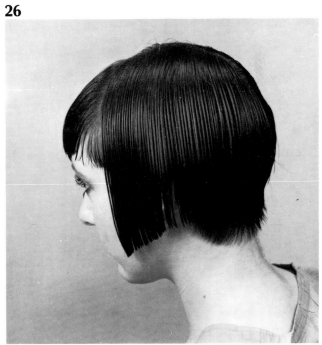

FIGS. 27, 28, 29, 30
Regard the total fringe as
a triangle. Cut fringe in
sections, as illustrated.
REMEMBER—THE HAIR
WILL LIFT ¼ in. WHEN
DRY, SO MAKE AN
ALLOWANCE FOR THIS.

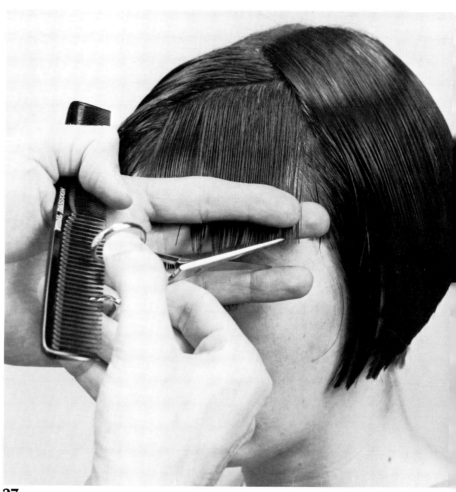

27

28

29 30

FIGS. 31, 32, 33, 34, 35, 36, 37, 38
Cross-checking
Cross-checking is an essential facet of the VIDAL SASSOON technique of hair cutting.
It involves lifting the hair away from the head in the opposite direction to which it has been cut, and checking for total accuracy, at the same time looking for any imperfections.
Cross-checking is the only way to achieve a totally precise and accurate result and should be regarded as an integral part of the cut.
IT SHOULD NEVER BE OMITTED!

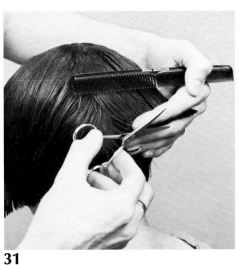 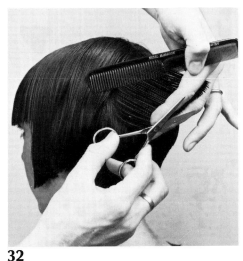 

31   32   33

33 · GRADUATED BOB ▷

34

35

36

37

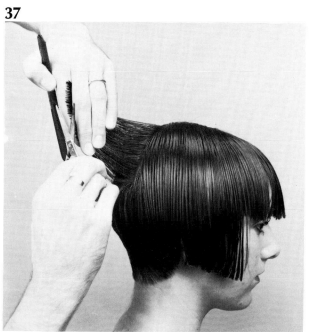

GRADUATED BOB · 34

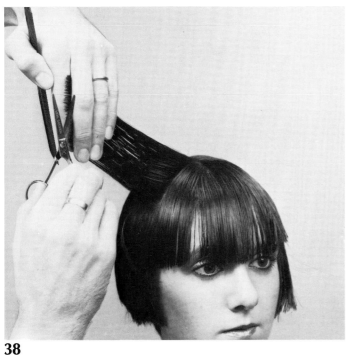

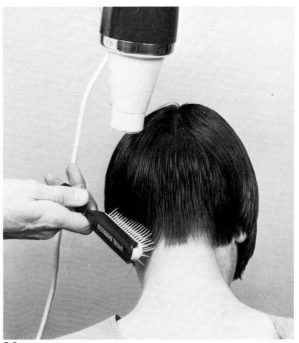

38

39

FIGS. 39, 40, 41, 42, 43, 44, 45
Drying
The cut produces the basic shape, and drying provides the finish.
Careful blow-drying will emphasise the smooth appearance and sheen of the hair.
Never hold the hand-dryer too close as excessive heat will damage the hair's condition and structure. The dryer should be moved slowly over the hair to ensure even application of heat.
Using a small brush start to blow dry at the back, drying the nape hair flat.
Taking small, even sections, work towards the top of the head and as the hair lengths get longer, change to a large brush. Lift the hair over the brush to achieve a bevelled smoothness, and to give body and bounce without too much curl.
The closer the brush is to the roots, the more 'lift' it gives to the hair—e.g. at the crown and fringe.
CAUTION: MAKE SURE EACH SECTION IS COMPLETELY DRY BEFORE MOVING ON TO THE NEXT.

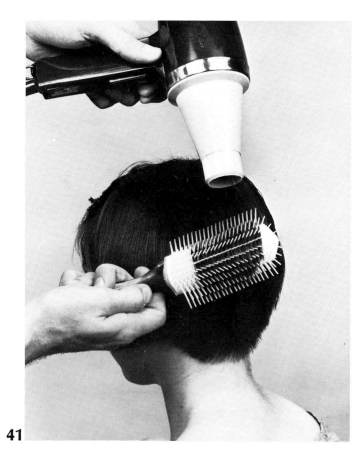

40

41

42

GRADUATED BOB · 36

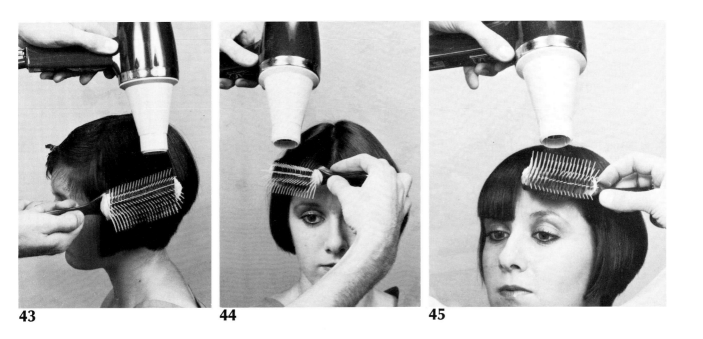

43   **44**   **45**

FIG. 46
The finished result.

THE CLASSIC BOB (1963)

A new era begins.
International recognition came for
Vidal Sassoon with this creation for
actress Nancy Kwan.
When it appeared in *Vogue* it made
front-page news all over the world.

THE FIVE-POINT CUT (1964)

The trade mark of Vidal Sassoon
which has never been equalled for its
absolute geometry. It was the perfect
complement to the clean-cut lines of
'The Swinging Sixties' fashions.

Cut 2

THE CLASSIC BOB

Gina is a colour technician at Vidal Sassoon in London. She knows that she must always be a first-class advertisement for her salon. Her dark red-brown hair is always beautifully conditioned and she wears her hair in this classic bob-shape to show off its glossy smoothness and natural swing. Gina's hair is heavy, with a regular texture, which is particularly suitable for this cut as it hangs so beautifully straight. The classic shape shows off her small, finely-cut features.

TOOLS REQUIRED:
Large scissors, comb, large brush, and hand-dryer.

1

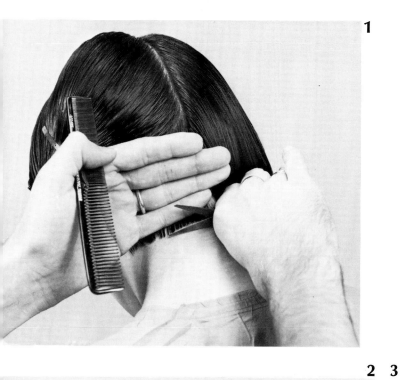

FIG. 1
Working as always on wet hair, make
a centre parting at the back.

2 **3**

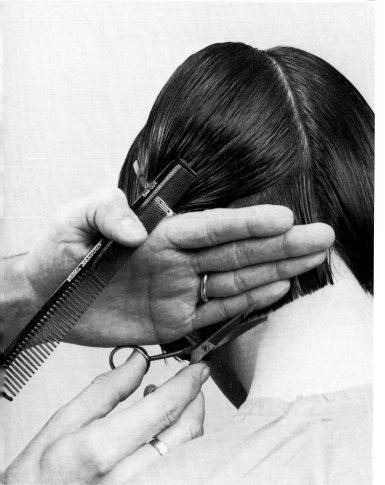

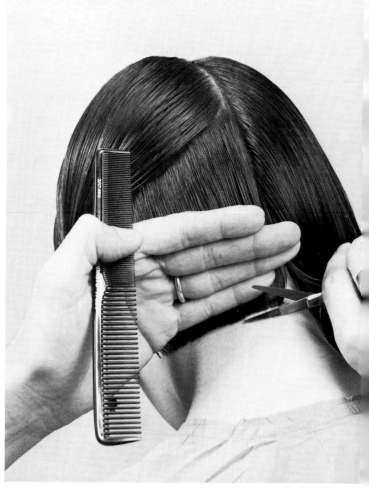

THE CLASSIC BOB · 42

4

FIGS. 2, 3, 4, 5, 6, 7
Secure the hair to one side at a downwards 45° angle. Comb down the first section and cut in the base line.
Comb each section down, hold firmly in place at the nape, and cut precisely, checking for loose ends, using the under-layers as a guideline. This will produce slight graduation, giving the finished haircut a bevelled appearance.

5

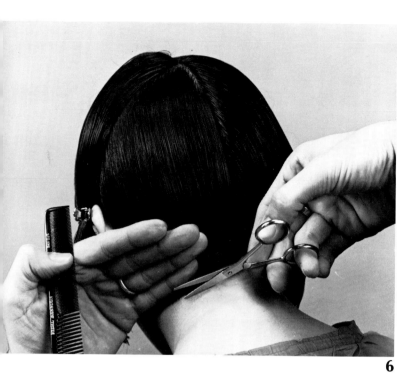

6

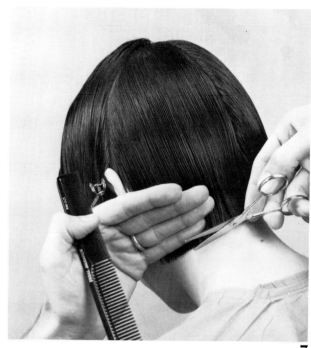

7

8

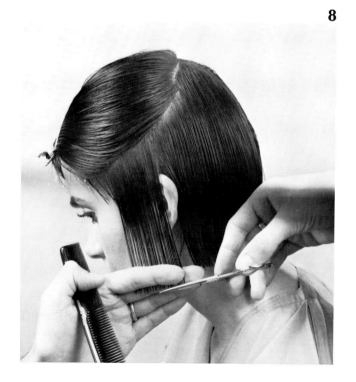

9

THE CLASSIC BOB · 44

10

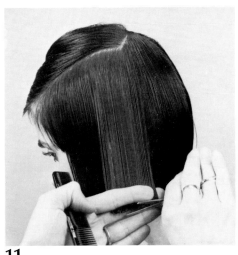

11

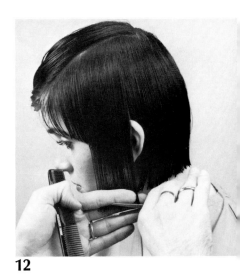

12

FIGS. 8, 9, 10, 11, 12, 13, 14, 15
Start at the side by holding the hair slightly away from the neck and follow the line through from the back. Holding the sections will produce the desired bevelled effect. Continue, taking clean, parallel sections, and work towards the top of the head.

13

14

15

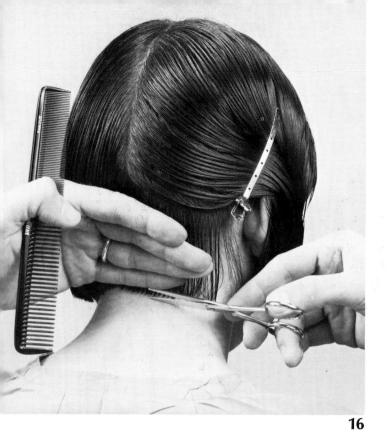

16

18

17

19

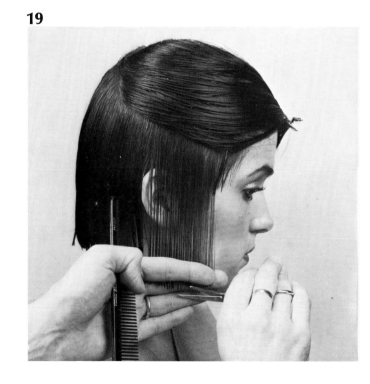

THE CLASSIC BOB · 46

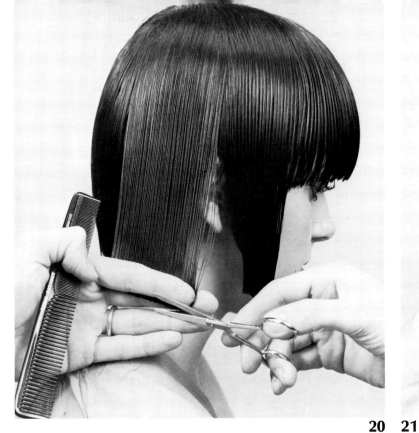

20 21

22

FIGS. 16, 17, 18, 19, 20, 21, 22
Halfway
Using the previously cut base-line as a guide, repeat the same technique for the second side.

23

24

25

FIGS. 23, 24, 25, 26, 27, 28, 29
Two techniques are used here to cut a deep fringe. Start by holding the hair *onto* the face to create a thick line, and, to get a softer effect in the centre, hold the hair *out* over the eyes.

26

27

28

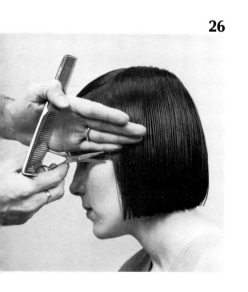

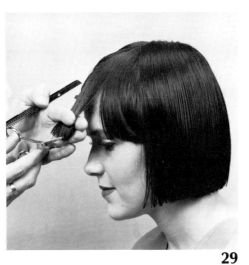 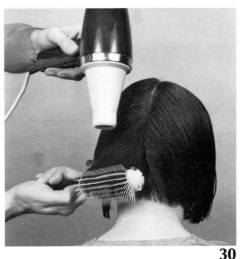 

29   30   31

FIGS. 30, 31, 32, 33, 34, 35, 36, 37, 38, 39, 40, 41, 42
Section off the hair for drying exactly as for cutting. Keep each section fine,
and blow-dry by directing gentle heat onto the brush as it moves through the
hair from roots to ends. Make sure each section is completely dry before
moving onto the next, but be careful not to over-dry or hold the dryer too
close.
Note: Always point the dryer towards the ends of the hair as this will flatten
the tiny cuticles on the hair shaft and produce maximum shine.

32   33   34

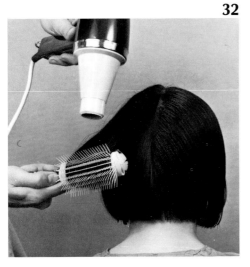 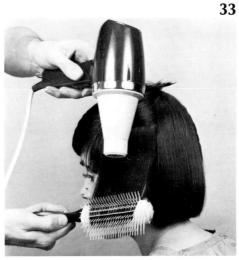 

35

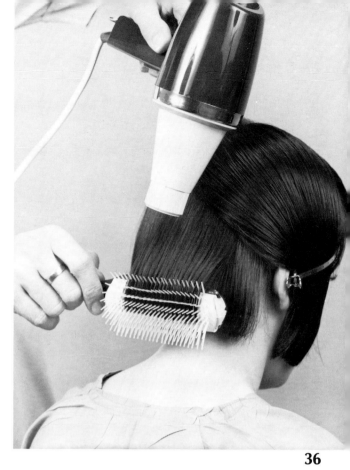

36

37

38

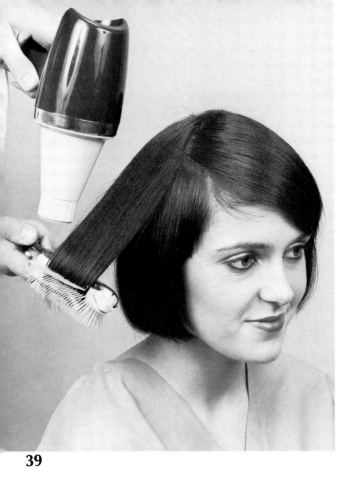

39

40

41

42

43

44

FIGS. 43 & 44
Two finished results from the same basic cut.

THE GEOMETRIC CUT (1965)

This was created to mark the opening of Vidal's first salon in America.

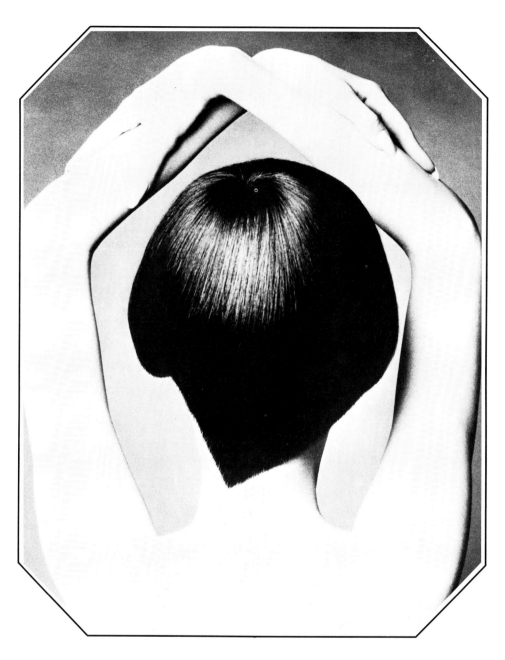

THE ASYMMETRIC CUT (1966)

Perfectly cut to follow the natural hairgrowth at the nape.

THE LONG GEOMETRIC CUT
(1966)

This look was introduced at the showing of Mila Schon's
collection in Rome.
The hair is cut short at the nape and long at the sides.
This line encourages the hair to swing freely and
precision cutting ensures that the hair falls perfectly
into shape.

Cut 3

THE HALO

Ann is a primary school teacher. She needed a casual, neat, and above all *practical* cut to see her through the rigours of her hectic days with the children and which falls naturally into place at all times. We advised her to have a 'Halo' cut—which will keep her in favour with the children and make a good impression on their parents!
The 'Halo' cut is very adaptable, as it lends itself equally well both to fine-textured and heavy hair.
The sloping line emphasised Ann's good cheekbones and attractive eyes.

TOOLS REQUIRED:
Small scissors, large and small brush, comb, and hand-dryer.

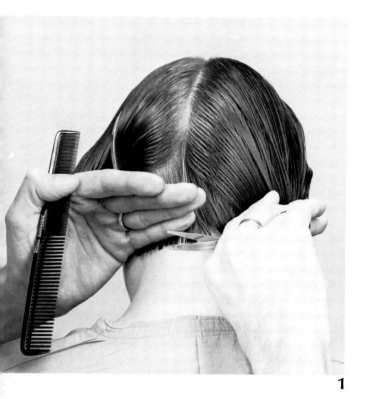

1

3

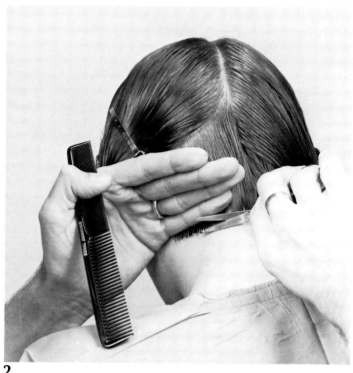

2

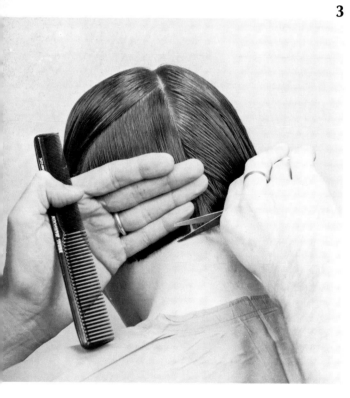

FIGS. 1, 2, 3, 4
From a centre parting, take a 45°
section to behind the ear. Comb
down first section, and cut in your
guide line, pressing the hair firmly
down on the skin. This gives a slight
graduated effect which complements
the roundness of this cut.
The second section is cut in exactly
the same way. This method is
continued for each section, working
towards the crown.

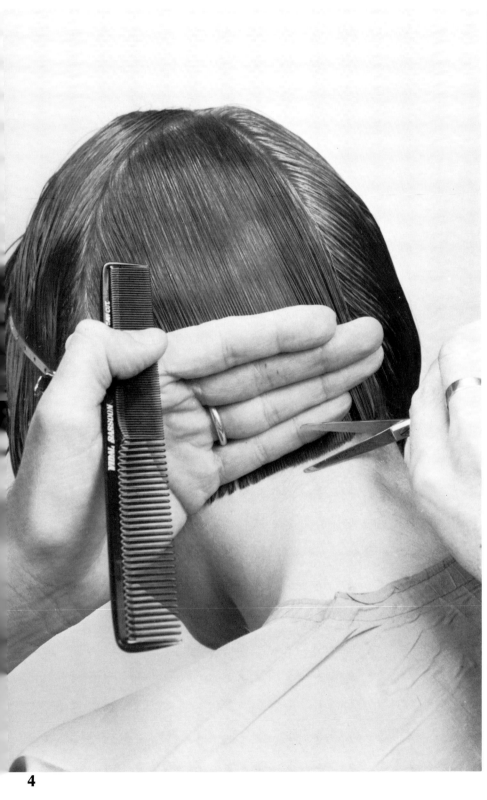

FIGS. 5 & 6
Holding the hair
gently but *firmly*, join
the hair at the side
into the line at the
back. Comb straight
down and cut shape
(Fig. 6).

4

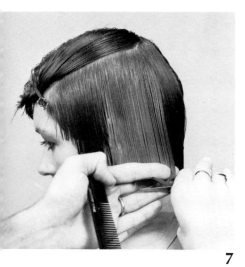

7

8

9

FIGS. 7, 8, 9, 10, 11
Build up the line by bringing down the remaining sections.
REMEMBER TO MAKE ALLOWANCES FOR EAR PROTRUSION!

10

11

12

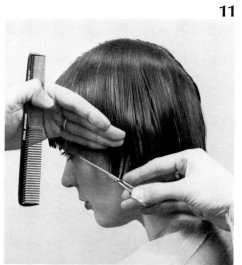

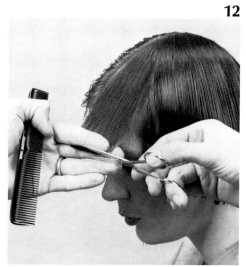

13

FIGS. 12, 13, 14
Cut the fringe from the crown,
joining into the side angle.

14

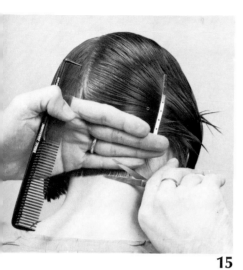

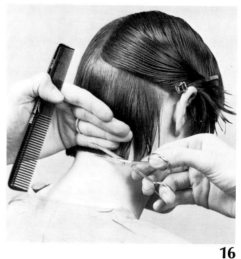

15   16   17

FIGS. 15, 16, 17, 18, 19, 20, 21, 22, 23
Halfway
Using the line and length of the left side as a guide, cut into the right side and continue as previously explained. Make absolutely sure that the lines correspond *exactly* on both sides—symmetry is vital in this cut.

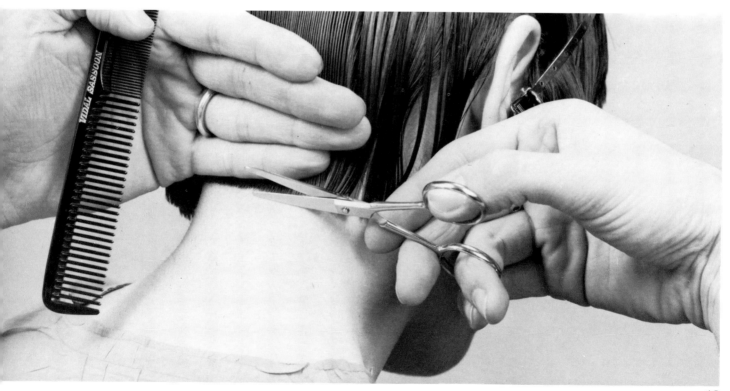

18

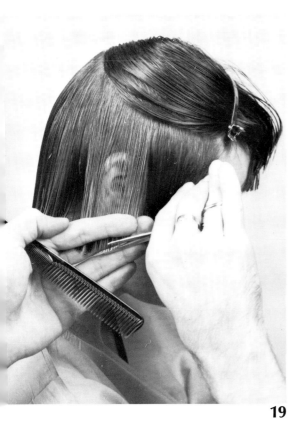

19

20

21

22

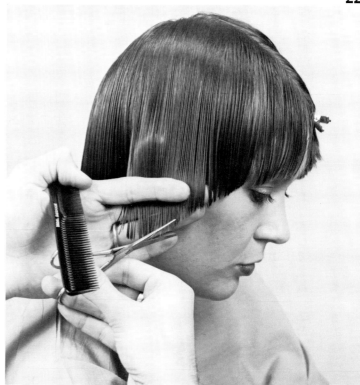

23

FIGS. 24 & 25 (opposite)
Make sure that the two sides of the
fringe blend and meet *exactly* in a
perfect line.

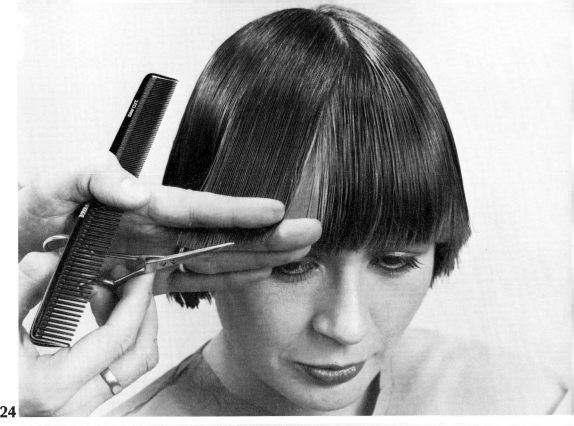

24

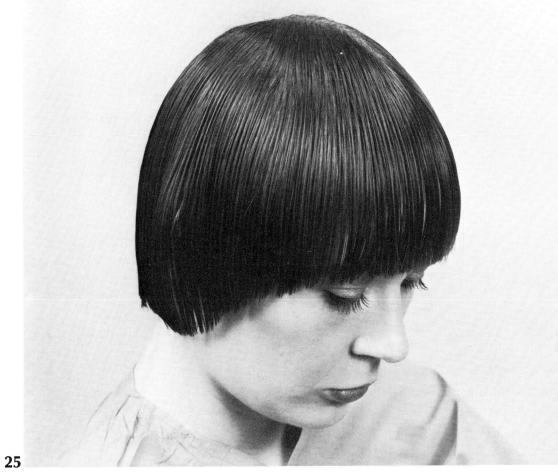

25

26

28

27

29

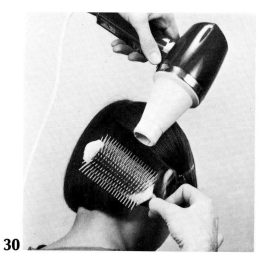

30

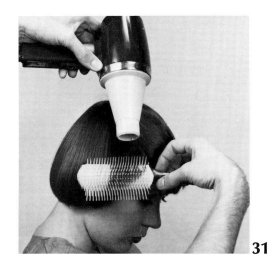

31

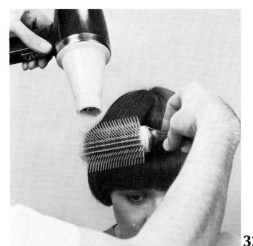

32

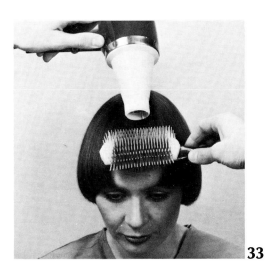

33

FIGS. 26, 27, 28, 29, 30, 31, 32, 33
Taking approximately the same
sections used during cutting, blow-
dry the short, underneath sections
with a small brush, changing to a
larger brush as the hair-lengths get
longer. This will help to achieve a
more rounded look.

FIG. 34
The finished result.

34

GREEK GODDESS (1967)

The Greek Goddess marked a major
step forward in Vidal's career and a
revolution in hairdressing.
He proved that by using his precision
cutting technique hair could be
permed and left to dry *naturally*.

ISADORA (1969)

A classic Vidal Sassoon 'long look'
inspired by the fluid movements of
Isadora Duncan's dancing.
The hair is encouraged to swing
freely by being cut in a sweeping line
from jaw-length to a heavy back.

THE MOUCHE (1969)

This cut was the first of Vidal
Sassoon's softer looks. The hair is
layered throughout and has long
wispy 'side-burns'.

THE SIGNATURE CUT (1970)

A short layered cut with longer
layers falling softly onto the face. The
VS has been stencilled onto the hair
and the front has been subtly
highlighted.

THE VEIL (1970)

A clever combination of very short
hair and very long hair. The short
hair is cut to create a 'cap' effect at
the crown and the long hair falls
freely over the shoulders. A long
wispy fringe covers the face.

HAVINGTON (1970)

A short layered haircut to
complement a beautifully shaped
head. Long soft tendrils help to
create a totally feminine look.

Cut 4

THE FIREFLY

Katherine is a secretary in a busy office, and needs
a neat, fashionable shape so that her hair can look
immaculate with the minimum of trouble and
she will always be a credit to her company—and
herself!

Katherine's hair is heavy with a slight natural 'bend'.
This type of hair, when cut, has a good deal of
volume, so that the shape is easy to maintain. The
'Firefly' cut which we have selected for her is
flattering to a wide variety of face shapes and is
particularly suitable for Katherine, who has a long,
slender neck and a very attractive jawline. The
width above the ears draws attention to the focal
point of her face—her lovely eyes.

TOOLS REQUIRED:
Small scissors, small and large brush, comb, and hand-dryer.

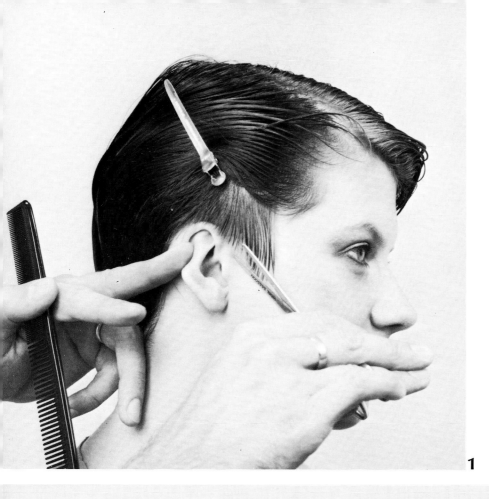

1

2

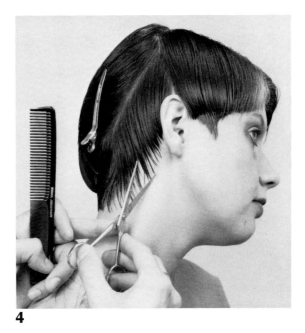

3 **4**

FIGS. 1, 2, 3

The first section (Fig. 1) is taken
above the ear, approximately parallel
with the hairline. Comb hair down
and cut.

The second section is taken from the
temple, gradually sloping down
towards the centre of the ear. Lift the
hair away from the head and direct
slightly forward. Cut parallel to the
angle of the section.

Continue taking sections up to the
parting. This procedure will create
both graduation and line.

FIGS. 4 & 5

Take a section parallel with the
hairline behind the ear, and cut the
outline before commencing
graduation.

5

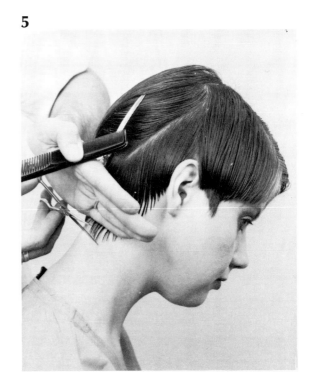

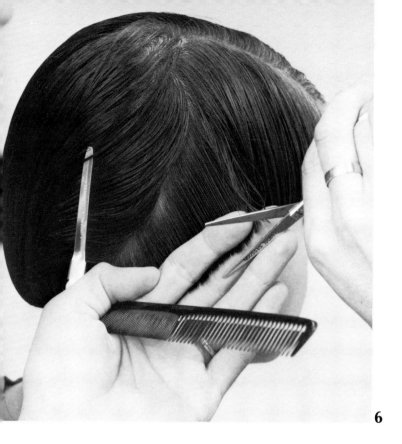

FIG. 6
Using a small section of the front as a guide, cut the hair, lifting it out and forward.

6

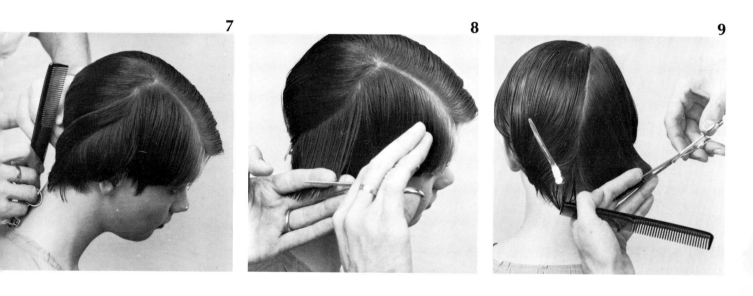

7   8   9

FIGS. 7, 8, 9
Continue graduating in small sections, working towards a centre parting.

THE FIREFLY · 78

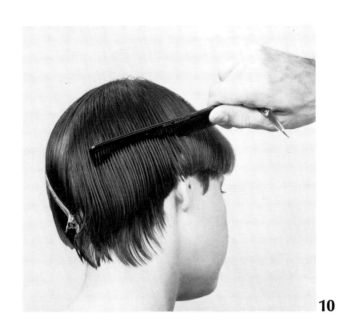

10

FIGS. 10, 11, 12
Comb down and back into shape, checking for uniformity in the graduation.

11

12

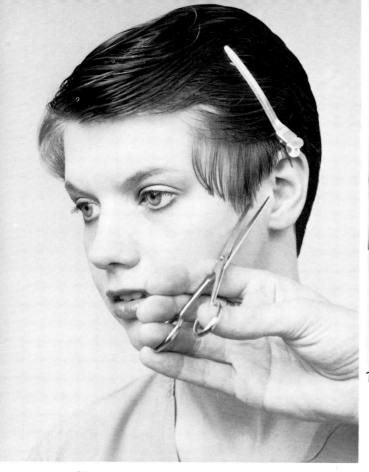

13

15

FIGS. 13, 14, 15, 16
Halfway
Continue cutting as before (Figs. 13 & 14). Pull the hair down, always directing it towards the face, using each previously-cut section as a guide (Figs. 15 & 16).
NOTE THE WIDTH OF SECTIONS.

14

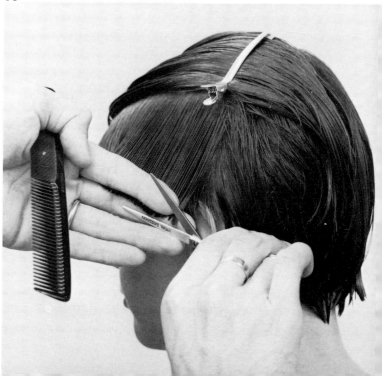

16

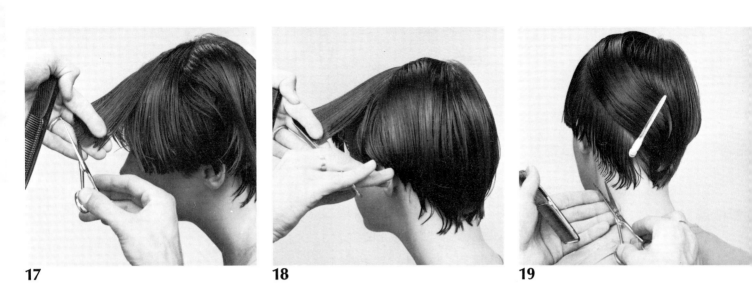

17   18   19

FIGS. 17, 18, 19, 20, 21, 22, 23, 24, 25, 26
Round off the leading edge of the front (Fig. 17). Continue graduation through
to the back as on the previous side (Fig. 18).
The method is exactly as used for the right side (Figs. 19, 20, 21, 22, 23, 24, 25,
26).

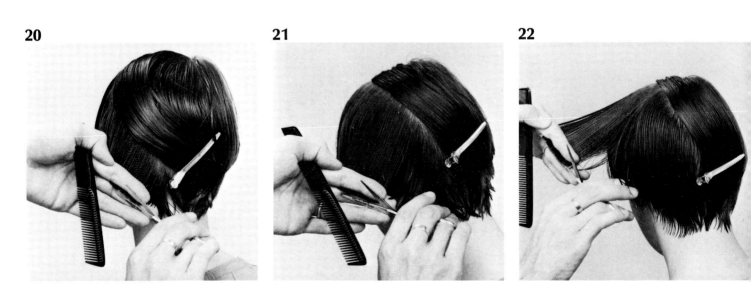

20   21   22

23

24

25

26

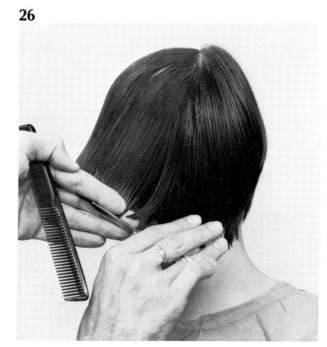

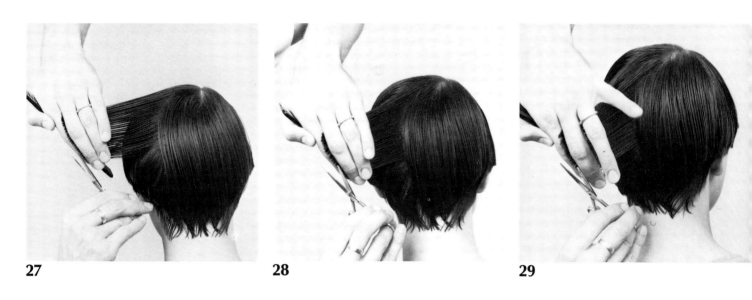

27

28

29

FIGS. 27, 28, 29, 30, 31
To cross-check this haircut, take fine vertical lines from behind the ear and
work towards the centre. Repeat on the opposite side.

30

31

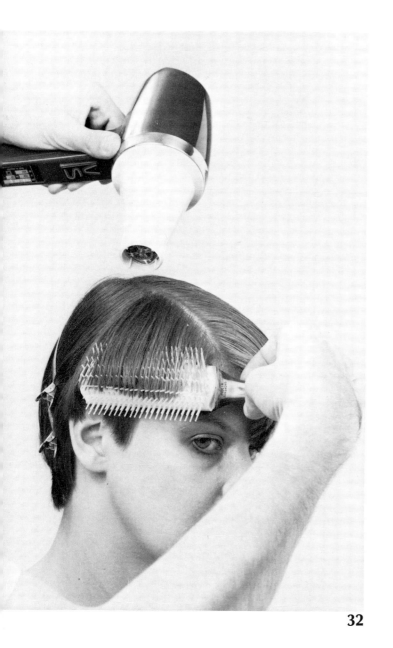

32

33

34

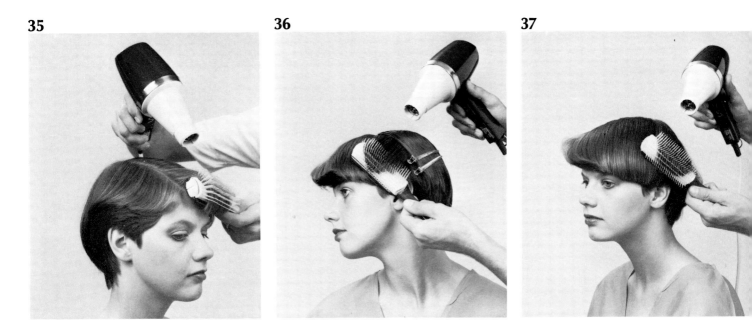

35   **36**   **37**

FIGS. 32, 33, 34, 35, 36, 37, 38, 39, 40
For this cut the hair should be blow-dried forward, section by section, until both sides are dry, and then brushed backwards.

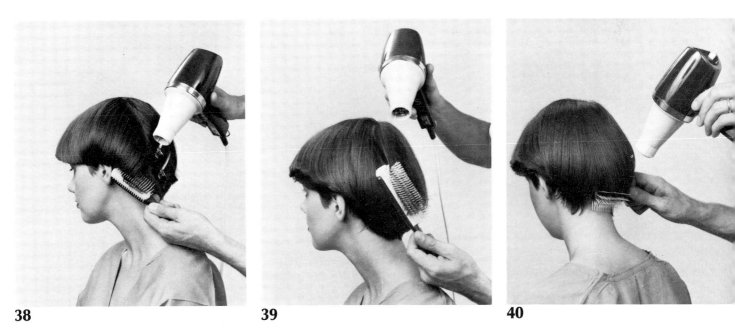

38   **39**   **40**

FIGS. 41 & 42
For the finishing touch, direct the hair round the brush to give a slight curve to the top sections.

41

42

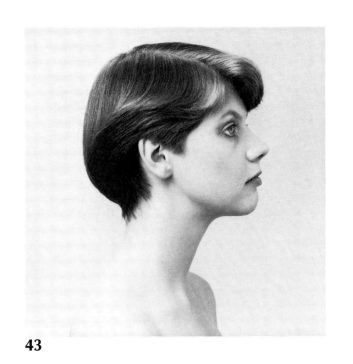

43

44

FIGS. 43 & 44
The finished result.

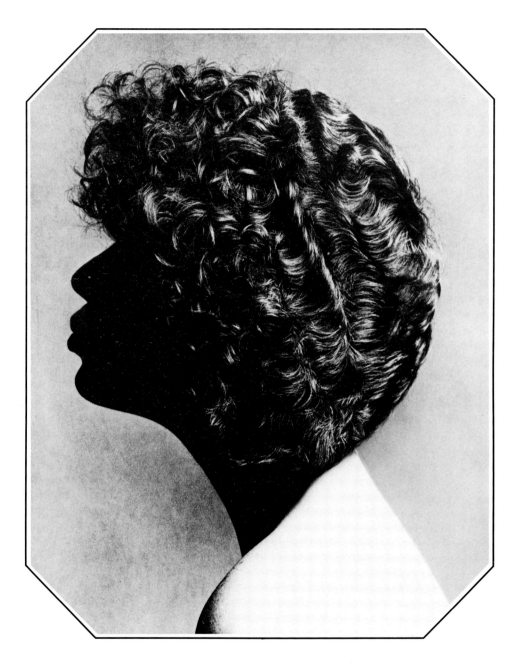

WASHBOWL (1971)

A beautifully rounded shape
achieved by brushing the hair
forward from the crown and leaving
the curls to fall naturally around the
face.

THE FALL (1972)

A fine one-length cut to emphasize healthy shining hair.
The fringe is extended across the ear and then the line
falls dramatically into the heavy length at the back.
This cut is particularly complementary to fine bone
structures.

BRUSH (1972)

This 'fun' look, inspired by a shaving brush, has been achieved by cutting a round shape on exceptionally thick spiky hair, which stands out naturally of its own accord.

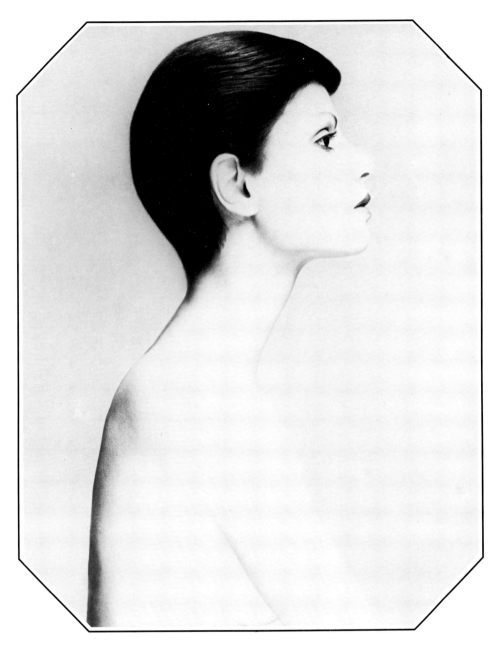

GIGI (1973)

A 'short back and sides' precision cut
that is brushed back smoothly over
the head. A perfect simple look that
enhances a delicate face and slender
neck.

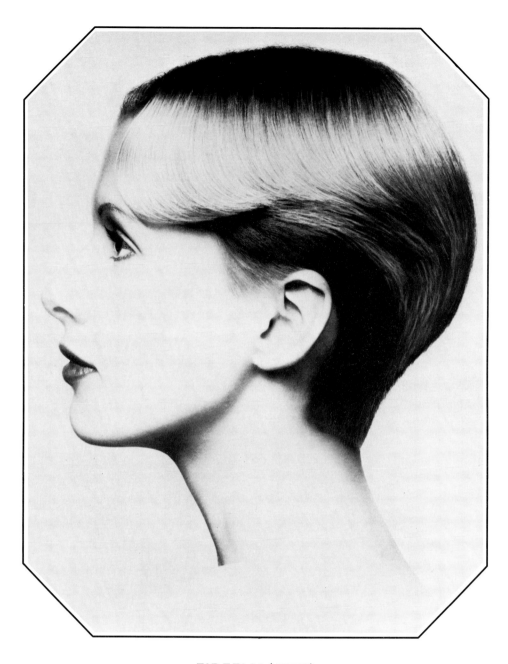

FIREFLY (1973)

The hair at the sides and nape is closely graduated with longer layers towards the top. The hair is brushed back over the ears from a centre parting.
To emphasize the dramatic change from short to long hair, the top layers are highlighted and the graduation underneath is darkened.

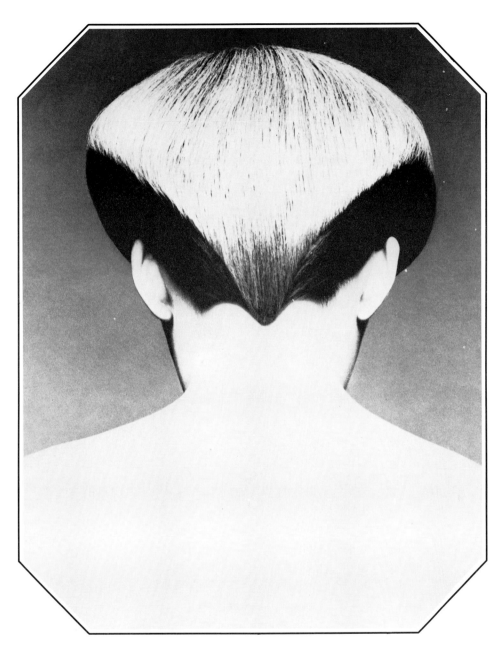

THE WEDGE (1974)

The object of the cut is to create a shape within a shape. The hair is cut to one length all over the head. The 3-dimensional effect is achieved by steep graduation underneath with the top layers brushed back into the nape of the neck making the 'wedge'.

Cut 5

THE SHORT BASIC CUT

Sue is a young student nurse with lots of outdoor interests. She wanted a 'no-fuss' haircut to fit in with her active life, to look good during her gruelling hours on the hospital wards as well as at parties and on the tennis court.

Sue has heavy, chunky hair which is very easy to manage. We chose for her a short basic cut, graduated onto the face to complement her best features.

TOOLS REQUIRED:
Small scissors, small and large brush, comb, and hand-dryer.

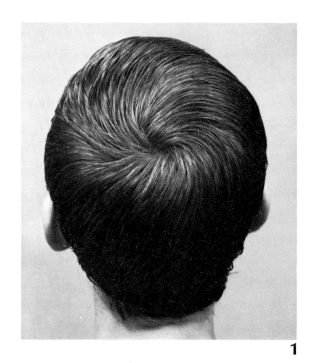

FIG. 1
First find the natural crown point.

FIGS. 2 & 3
Part the hair down the centre. Take a small section from the parting to behind the ear. Cut the base-line.

1

2

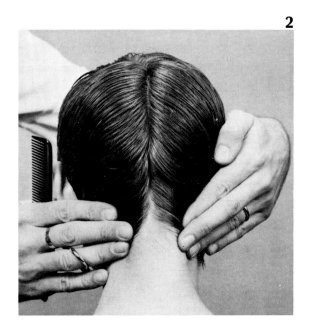

3

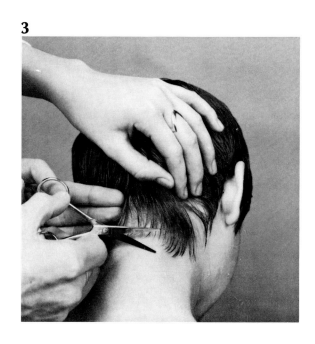

THE SHORT BASIC CUT · 96

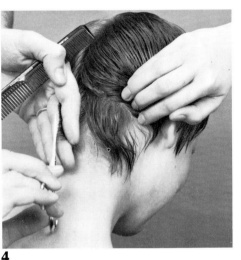

4

5

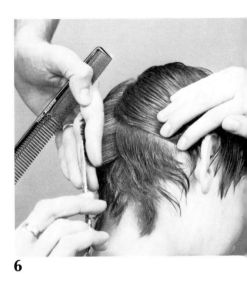

6

FIGS. 4, 5, 6, 7, 8
Using the base-line as a guide, begin working vertically up towards the occipital bone. Hold the hair at a 45° angle (Figs. 4 & 5).
Taking clean sections, incline the knuckles *towards* and the fingertips *away* from the head. This method achieves a flat graduation (Figs. 6, 7, 8).

7

8

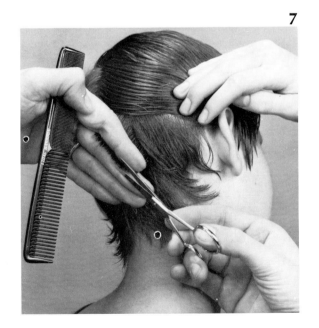

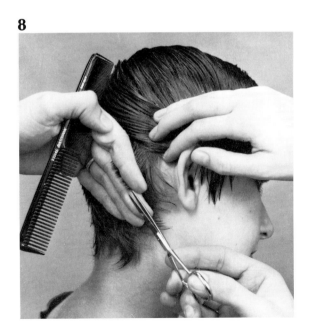

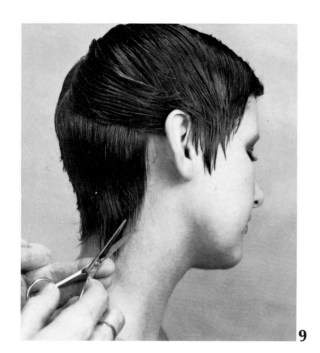

FIG. 9
Take a horizontal section, comb the hair down, and cut the line behind the ear.

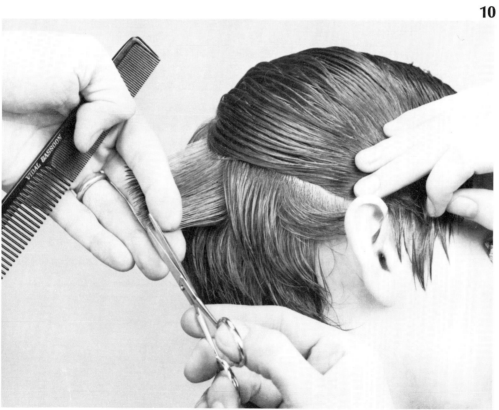

THE SHORT BASIC CUT · 98

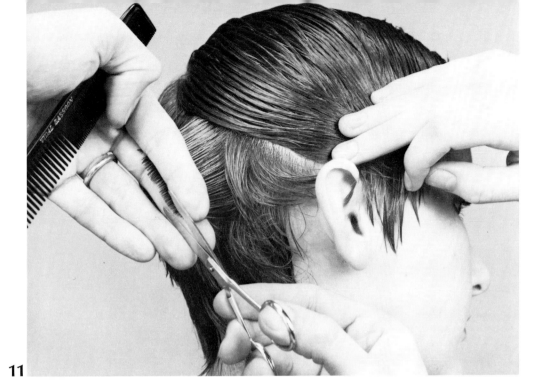

11

12

FIGS. 10, 11, 12
Using the previously-cut lengths as a guide, follow the spherical shape of the skull up from the occipital bone to the crown (Fig. 12).

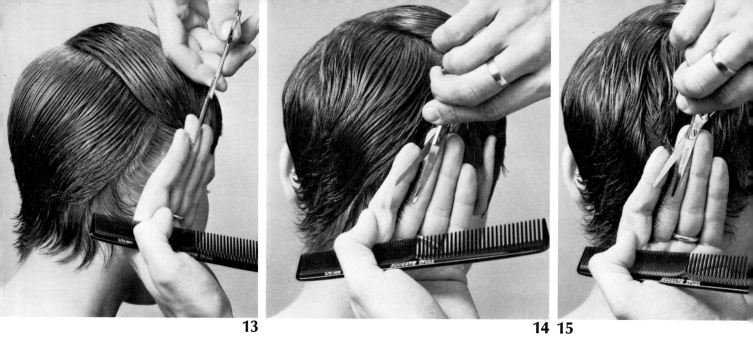

13   **14 15**

FIGS. 13, 14, 15, 16, 17
On a layered cut, checking should not be left to the end. Check the sections which have just been cut, starting behind the ear and working towards the centre.

16   **17**

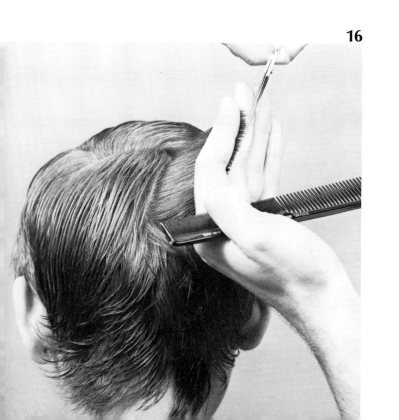
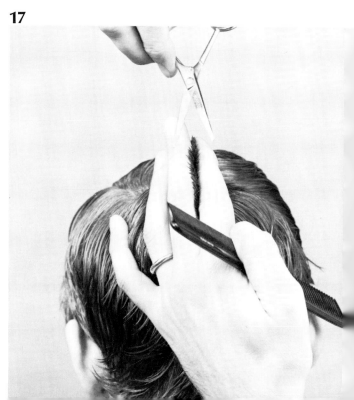

FIGS. 18 & 19
Take a horizontal section
approximately 1 in. above the ear,
comb down, and cut the shape
across the ear.

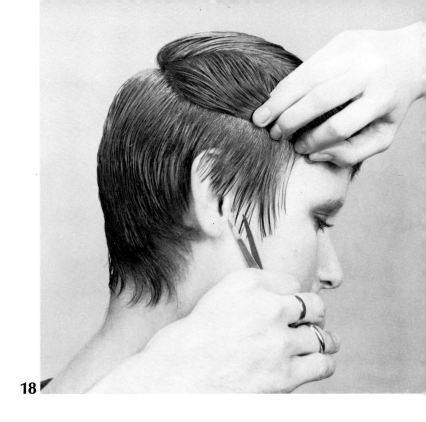

18

19

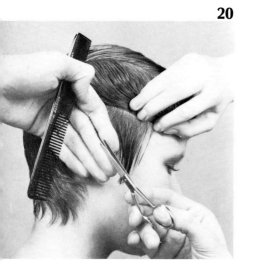  

FIGS. 20, 21, 22, 23, 24
Using the outline shape as a guide, take vertical sections and angle the fingers as before to obtain flat graduation. Work through until reaching a section on an approximate level with the pupil of the eye.

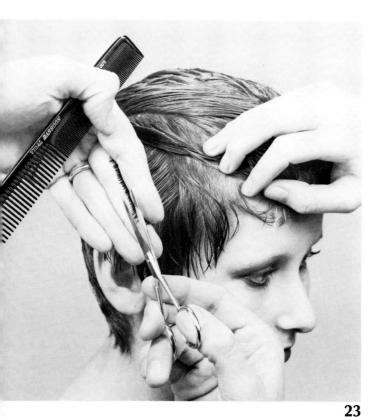 

23 **24**

FIGS. 25 & 26
Check the sections which have just
been cut, working back from the
face line.

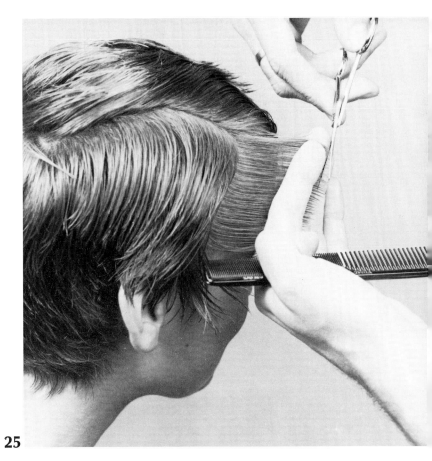

25

26

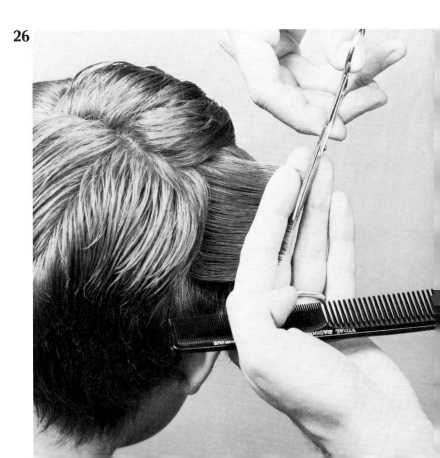

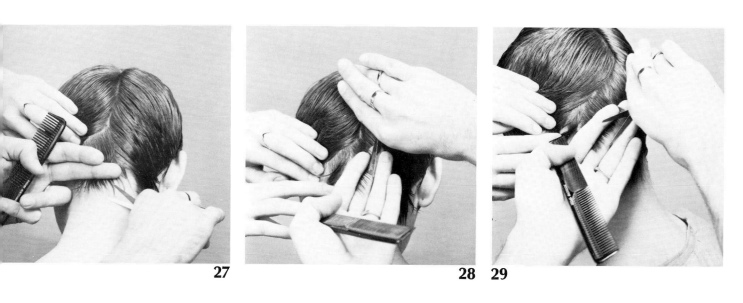

27   28 29

FIGS. 27, 28, 29, 30, 31, 32
Halfway
Commence work on the left side. Use the same method and order of
procedure as used on the right side.

30   31 32

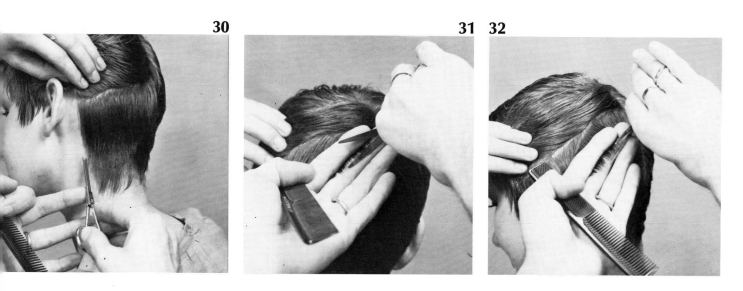

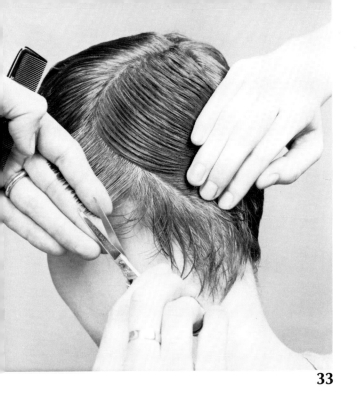

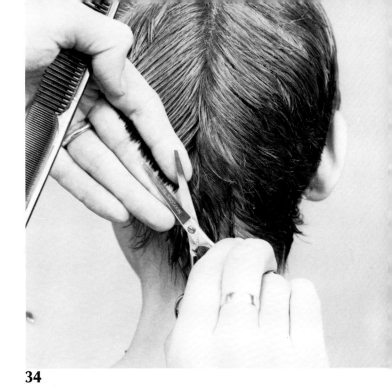

33

34

FIGS. 33, 34, 35
Check the back, as illustrated.

35

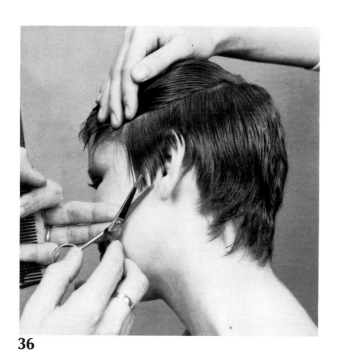

36

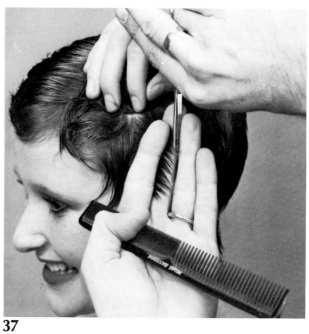

37

38

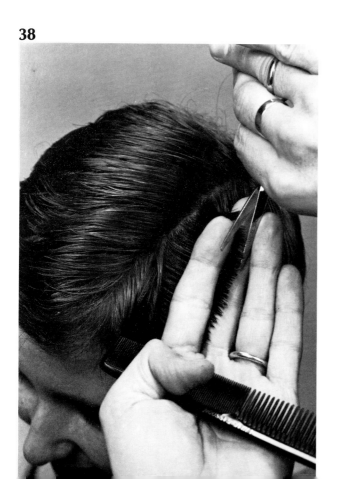

FIGS. 36, 37, 38
When cutting the second side, refer to the mirror to ensure that continuity of the shape is being achieved.

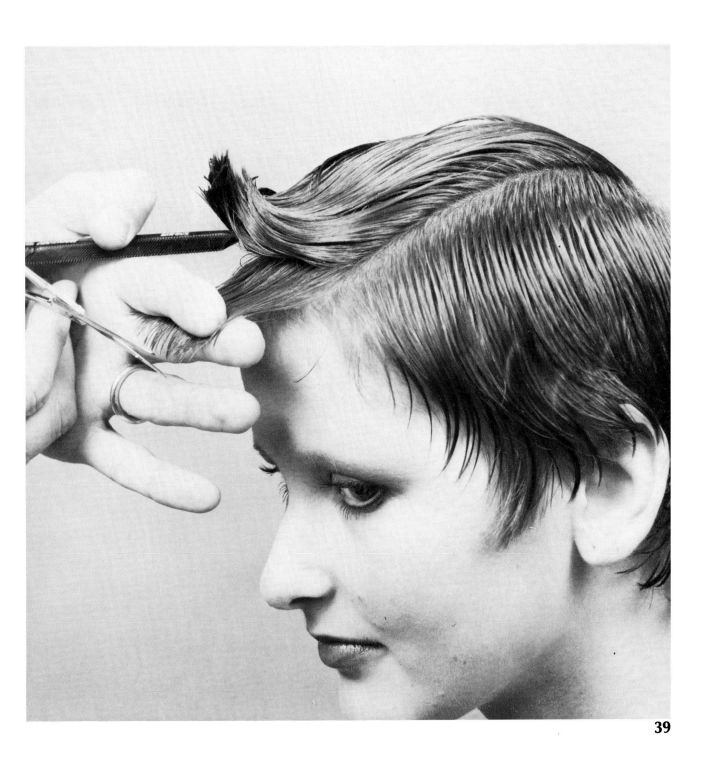

FIG. 39
Cut the fringe to desired length.

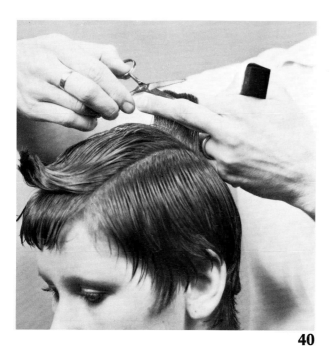

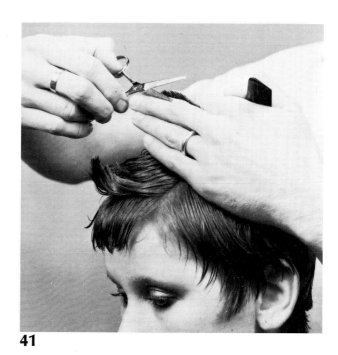

40 **41**

FIGS. 40, 41, 42, 43
Using the hair which has been cut at the crown as a guide, take narrow, horizontal sections, hold them at a slightly forward angle, and cut across squarely.
Follow through to the fringe.

42 **43**

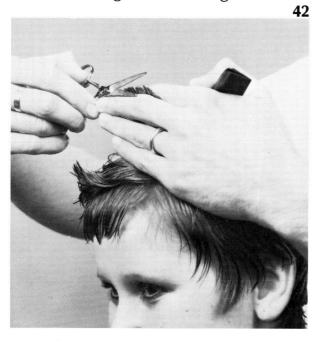

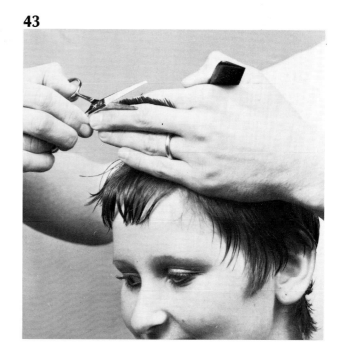

FIGS. 44 & 45
Lifting sections vertically, cross-check the top.

46   **47**

48

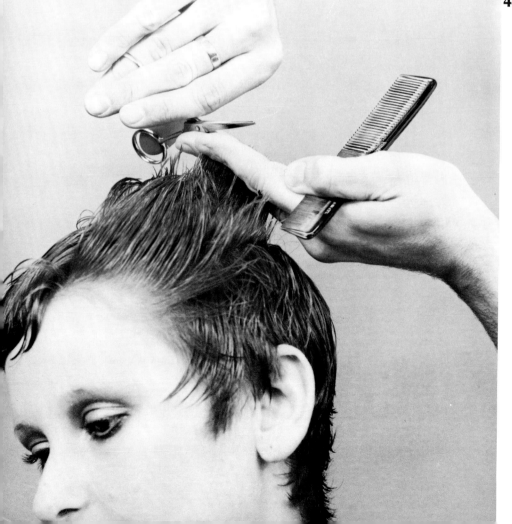

49 **50**

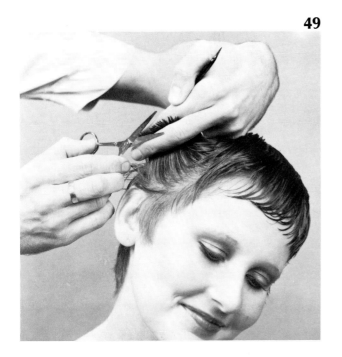 

FIGS. 46, 47, 48, 49, 50, 51, 52, 53, 54, 55
Cross-check through the whole head for uniformity of shape and graduation.

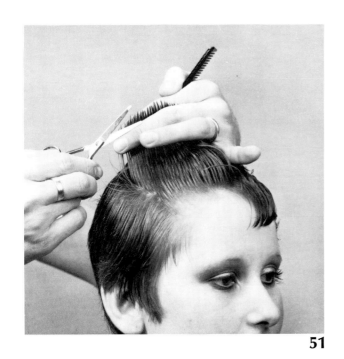 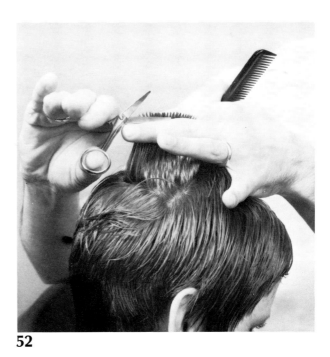

51 **52**

53   54 55

FIGS. 56, 57, 58, 59, 60, 61, 62, 63, 64, 65, 66, 67
Hair is dried softly following the shape of the cut and the head. Keep the dryer and brush moving in a smooth, free-flowing motion.
Use a large brush for shaping and a small brush for volume and finish.

56   57 58

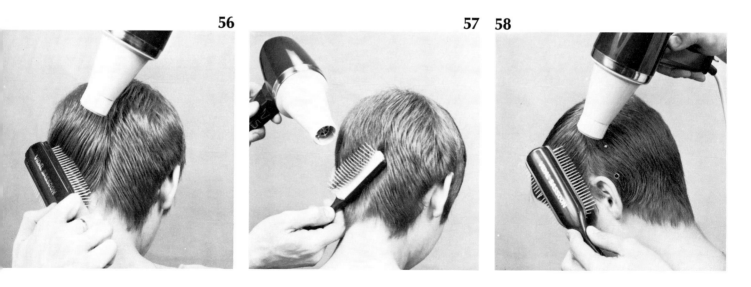

THE SHORT BASIC CUT · 112

59 **60**

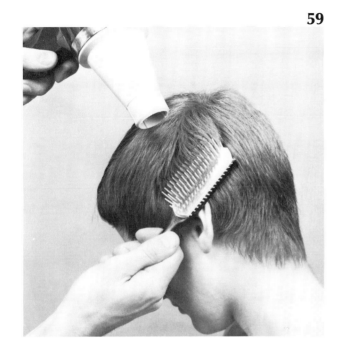 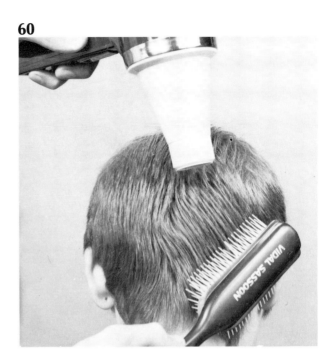

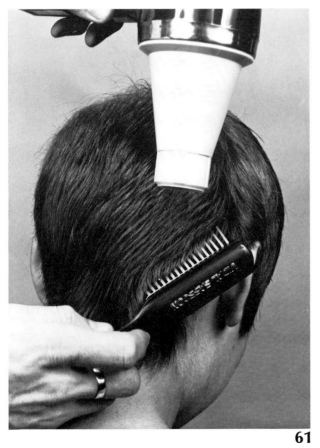 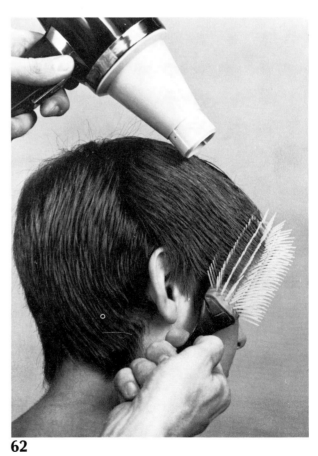

61 **62**

63

64

65

66

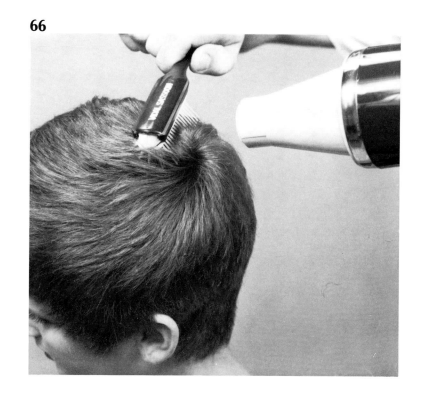

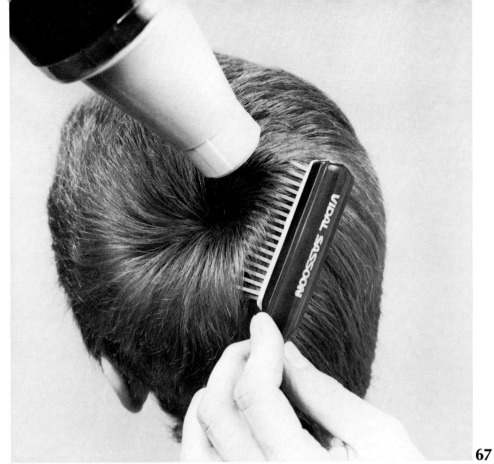

67

68

FIG. 68
The finished result.

CADETTE (1980)

Short and sharp with a touch of softness – that's the
Sassoon story for the Eighties. A bold, clean cut,
geometric outline with plenty of Eighties texture
achieved by precision layering. The shiny condition of
the hair is maintained with the regular use of the Vidal
Sassoon Hair Care range.

116

BOTTICELLI (1974)

An unusual and totally new look created by combining, for the first time, permed and straight hair. Only the ends are permed forming a soft volume of curls all round.

DARK LADY (1974)

Another interesting look featuring a combination of permed and straight hair. A different perming technique is used here to create a 'straighter' volume of hair. The crown and fringe are left naturally smooth and glossy with a side comb drawing the hair away from the face and forming an eye-catching feature.

118

ERTÉ (1974)

Inspired by and dedicated to the exotic designs of Erté, this cut was created to celebrate the publication of Erté's autobiography *Things I Remember*. Shiny dark hair is slicked forward and cut into half-moon shapes joining at a point above the eyes. Thus, the contrasting pale face takes on a perfect heart shape. Notice how the skilful use of make-up enhances the effect.

Cut 6

THE GREEK GODDESS

Jackie is an air hostess, with a busy, erratic schedule. She wanted a cut that would look good at any hour of the day or night, one that she could look after herself and that she could rely on to look perfect, however short the notice.
We picked for her a permed version of the 'Short Basic Cut'. This is excellent for fine hair, and gives Jackie the slight extra volume required to balance her jawline. The hair is towel-dried, combed, and left to dry naturally. A real cut for ladies in a hurry!

TOOLS REQUIRED:
Small scissors, comb. The hair is left to dry naturally. (A heat lamp may be used for fast drying.)

This cut requires exactly the same technique as
Sue's basic cut (page 94).
Jackie's hair has been permed to achieve a natural
curly appearance. The hair is left to dry naturally
and pushed into shape with the fingers if required.

CORRINNE (1979)

Corrinne is an asymetric graduated haircut using the
round graduation technique, eliminating the parting.
Colour Slices (that is using a similar technique to
Highlighting, but instead of lightening a weaved section,
a fine solid section is lightened) have also been used to
accentuate the haircut.

THE BERET (1975)

Inspired by the French workman's beret, this easy-to-wear cut falls in heavy layers from the crown.

ROSSETTI (1975)

A stunning pre-Raphaelite look
created for naturally curly hair. The
hair is parted in the centre, cut into
heavy layers to produce maximum
width and volume, and left to dry
naturally. The same look can be
achieved with permed hair.

Cut 7

AFRO CUT

Christina is a photographic model, and her hair is very important to her work.

'Afro' hair, although it may look thick and wiry, is in fact very fine, with a soft texture, so we decided to create for her a rounded shape, maximizing the volume and emphasizing the natural spring.

N.B. The utmost care must be taken when cutting Afro-type hair, as one false step will destroy the symmetry of the shape.

TOOLS REQUIRED:
Large scissors, Afro comb.

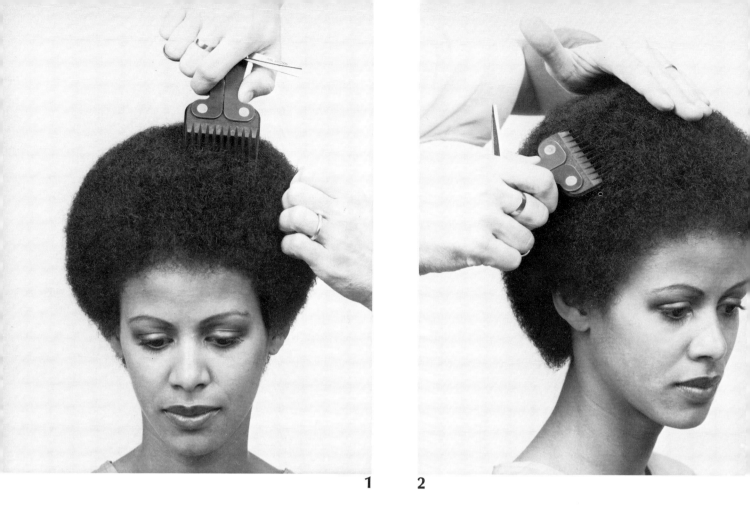

1   2

FIGS. 1 & 2
Shampoo the hair and let it dry naturally. Cut when it is *dry*.
Start by lifting the hair out with a wide-toothed comb. Do not stretch the hair
beyond its natural elasticity.

3

4

FIGS. 3, 4, 5, 6
The hair is shaped working from the front using a free-hand cutting method.
Slowly begin to 'carve' the shape in. Be aware constantly of balance between
emerging hair shape and bone structure.

5   6

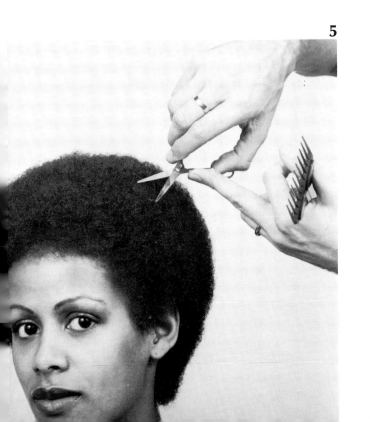

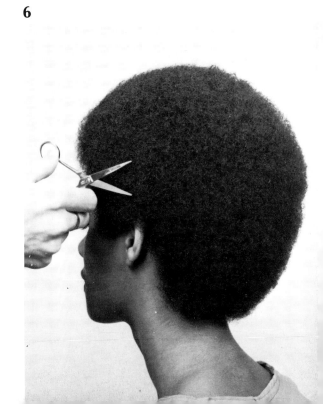

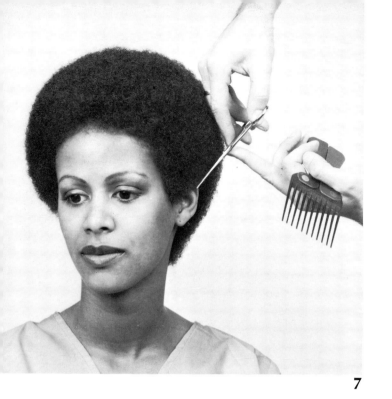

7   8

FIG. 7
Cut the shape across the ear.

9

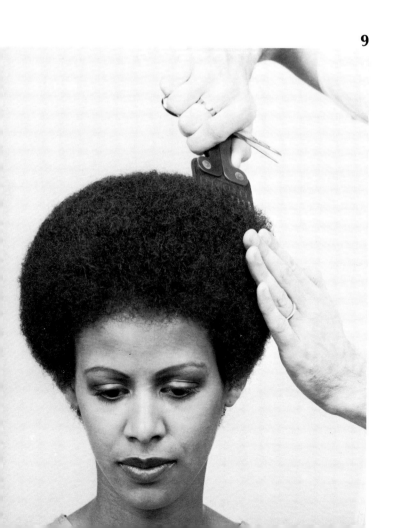

FIGS. 8, 9, 10
Work through the hair, occasionally pulling it up with the wide-toothed comb to check for uniformity.
Bear the overall shape constantly in mind. Keep working at it, gradually reducing it, and controlling the volume.

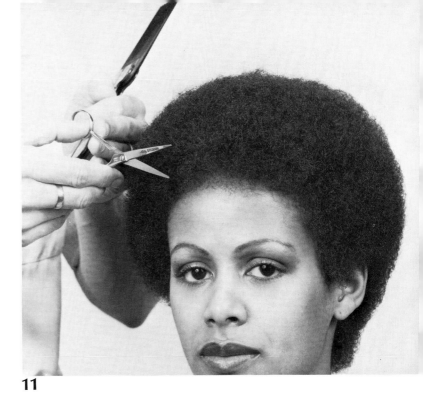

10   11

FIG. 11
Refer frequently to the mirror to check that balance is being maintained.

12

FIGS. 12, 13, 14, 15
Halfway
Again, begin at the ear and continue to the top, building up the round shape.

13   14

15

FIGS. 16, 17, 18, 19
The roundness at the back is formed
using the same free-hand method.
Remember to keep lifting the hair
out with the comb. This must be
done with regularity throughout
cutting.
A final all-over lift with the wide-
toothed comb will give maximum
volume and definition to the shape.

16

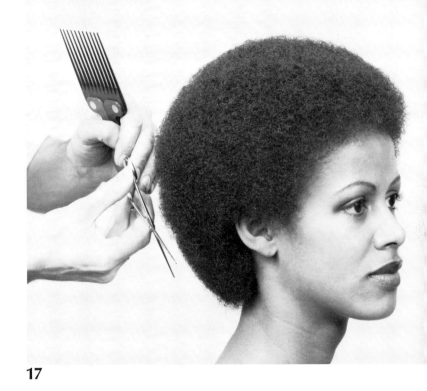

17

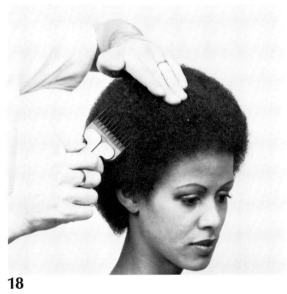

18

19

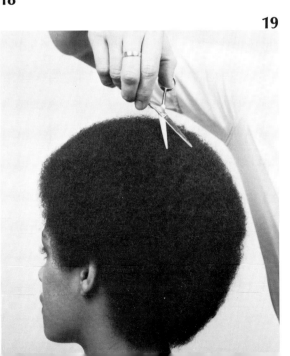

FIG. 20
The finished result.

20

133 · AFRO CUT

URCHIN (1979)

Short, touselled and sexy. One of the new variations of
the Vidal Sassoon theme for Spring 1980, the Textured
Asymmetrics.
A dramatic cut softened with the use of the most gentle
of perms to set off the new bolder make-up colours and
fashion styles.

POLKA (1980)

This is the softest version of the new Advanced Geometric
theme from the Vidal Sassoon Creative Team. Geometrics
are back – with a difference. The bold, clean shapes are
now often softened with precision layering and the lightest
of perms. Colour plays a very important role. The hair
is given volume, depth and interest with the use of the
new Vidal Sassoon 'Spotlighting' technique.

Cut 8

THE SHORT SHAKE

Juliette is a dancer and she likes her natural chestnut-coloured hair to move in unison with her dance movements. 'The Short Shake' cut is perfect for her thick, bouncy hair, as it will always fall back into place.

TOOLS REQUIRED:
Small scissors, comb, vent brush (for natural drying).

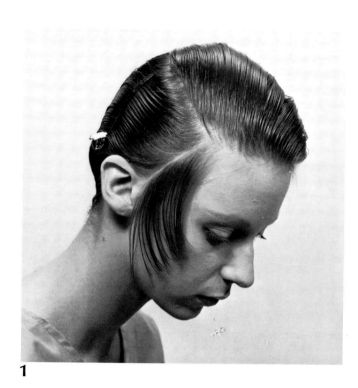

1

FIGS. 1, 2, 3, 4
Section off the side area. Take a
1 inch wide vertical section and
comb hair forward (Fig. 1).
Hold hair firmly between fingers,
directed outwards as shown (Fig. 2).
Take another section. Lift the hair
out and forward and cut at the same
angle as the previous section, using
this as a guide. Remember to keep
the hair well forward as this will help
to achieve more volume at the back
(Figs. 3 & 4).

2 **3** **4**

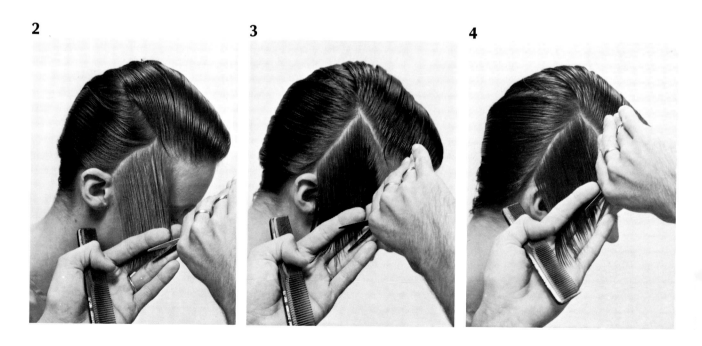

THE SHORT SHAKE · 138

FIGS. 5, 6, 7, 8
Section as shown (Fig. 5).
Comb the hair down into its natural
direction (Fig. 6).
Lift the hair between fingers, use the
line behind the ear as a guide.
Continue to lift out and cut sections
at this angle (Fig. 7).
Cut length line (Fig. 8).

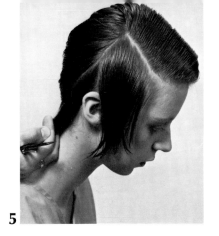

5

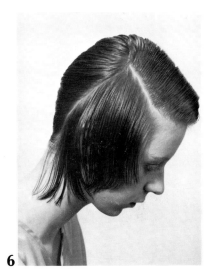

6

7

8

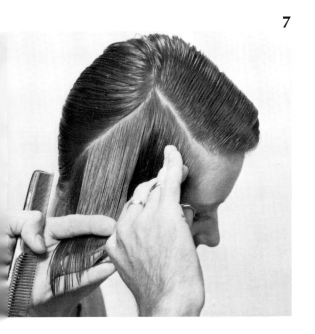

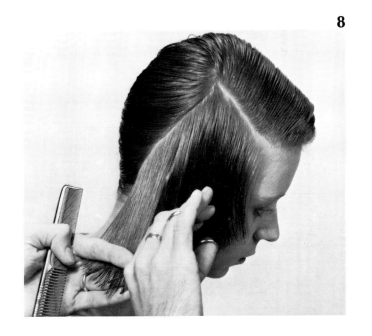

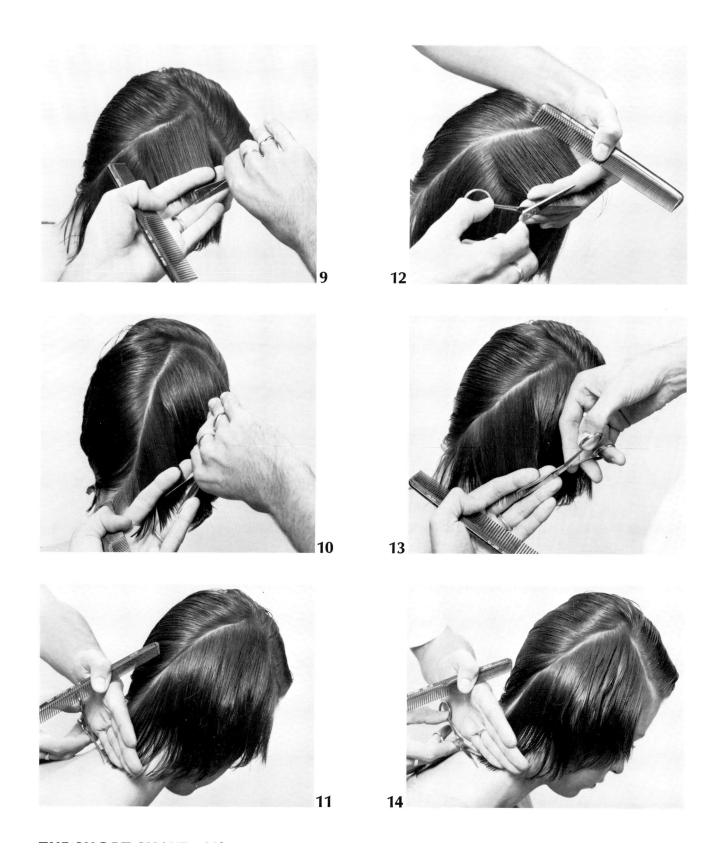

9

12

10

13

11

14

THE SHORT SHAKE · 140

FIGS. 9, 10, 11, 12, 13, 14
Take a section parallel to the previous one, directing the hair forward, and cut as shown (Fig. 9).
Continue the graduation down the section to the length line (Fig. 10).
Comb the hair down and check into length line (Fig. 11).
Continue cutting sections in this way until the centre parting is reached (Figs. 12, 13, 14).

16

FIGS. 15 & 16
Halfway
As before, section off side area and cut (Figs. 15 & 16).

15

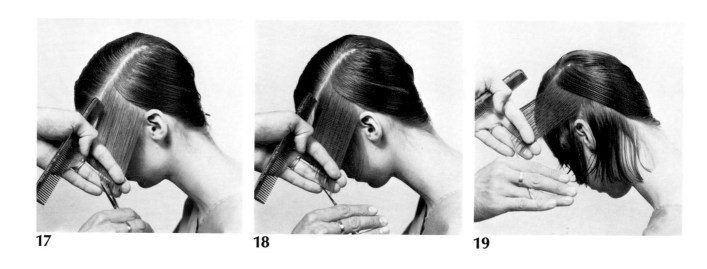

17   18   19

FIGS. 17, 18, 19, 20, 21
Continue graduating in sections, remembering to keep the hair well forward.

20   21

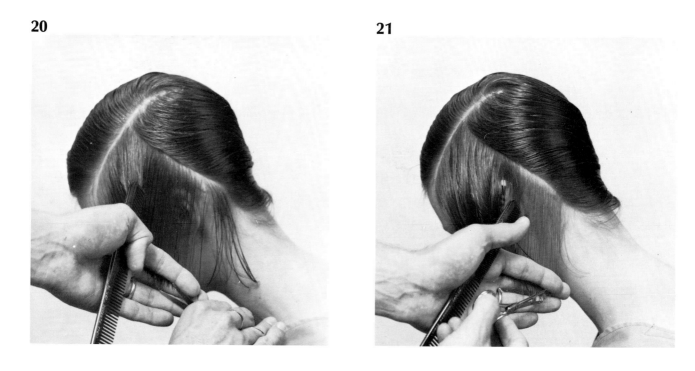

THE SHORT SHAKE · 142

22   23   24

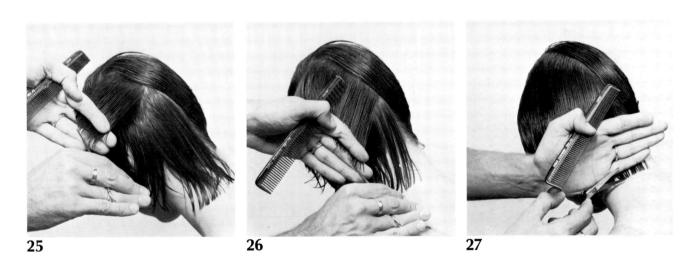

25   26   27

FIGS. 22, 23, 24, 25, 26, 27
Work across from behind the ear towards the centre using the previously cut section as a guide.

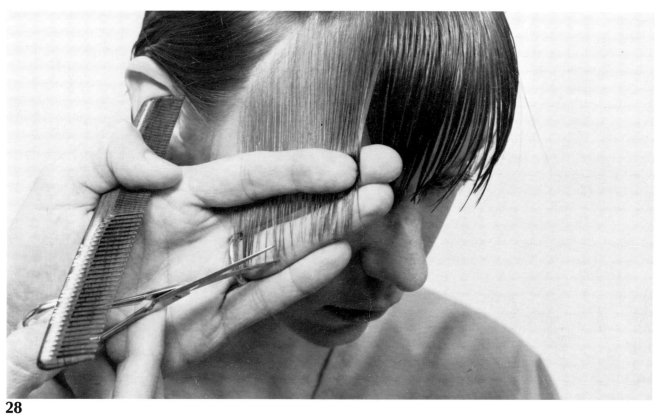

28

29

THE SHORT SHAKE · 144

 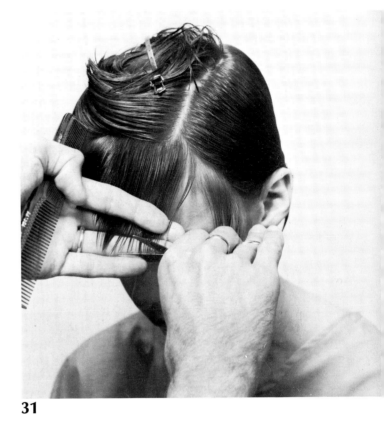

30 **31**

FIGS. 28, 29, 30, 31
Cut the top area last. Hold the first section forward, taking in a little of the side area with the fringe (Figs. 28 & 29).
Repeat on the other side, joining the two areas together (Figs. 30 & 31).

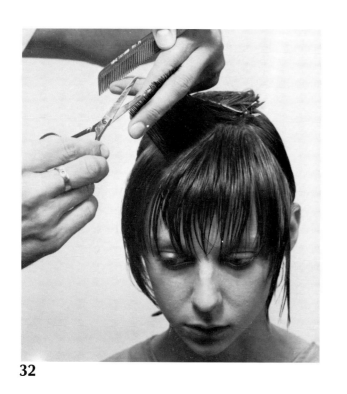

32

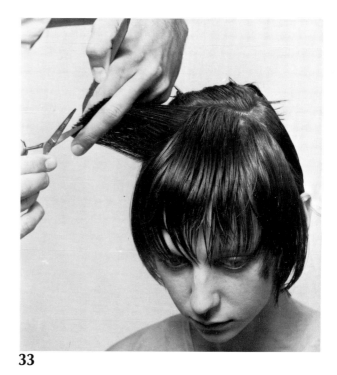

33

34

35

THE SHORT SHAKE · 146

FIGS. 32, 33, 34, 35, 36, 37
Work from the front towards the crown in parallel sections. Hold the hair up and slightly forward. Cut, checking into previous section (Figs. 32–37).

36

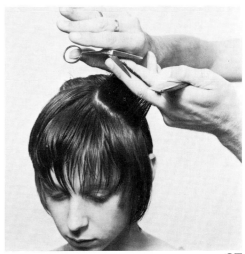

37

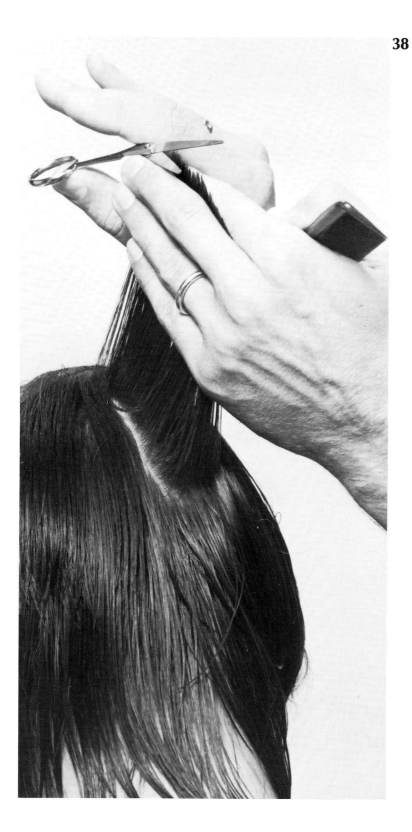

FIGS. 38, 39, 40
Cross-check to ensure that
all angles are perfectly even
(Figs. 38, 39, 40).

41

Drying
If the hair has the right texture, i.e. if it is thick and bouncy like our model's hair, it can be brushed forward into shape and left to dry naturally.
Fine, limp hair should be blow-dried, brushing the hair forward to give it more volume.

FIG. 41
The finished result.

JAP (1977)

An exotic look created from a simple
box bob.
The hair has been plaited when wet,
dried and then brushed out for a
'thatched' effect. Fine tendrils fall
over one eye to soften the look.

CAPULETTE (1979)

Capulette is an asymetric graduated haircut where the renowned Flying Colours technique (that is painting colour on to the hair so that the lighter sections appear closer to the eye than the darker sections) has been used to heighten the effect of the movement in the hair.

THE CURLY SHAKE (1977)

The perfect cut for the naturally
curly or permed hair. It is cut
upwards from the nape with long
layers left at the side and fringe to
frame the face. The hair is dried
naturally with the fingers.

PAMPAS (1982)

The hair was cut with round graduation from the temples coming up to the longest part. The back was layered quite close whilst trying to keep as much length as possible. The emphasis being on variation in both length and texture.

Cut 9

THE CURLY SHAKE

Fay is an actress, specializing in repertory, and so she is constantly on the move; she therefore needs a versatile cut, the look of which she can change for any part.
We chose for her a soft, longer-length cut, capitalizing on the natural curl and attractive texture of her hair.

TOOLS REQUIRED:
Short scissors, comb, and large comb.
N.B. A large comb is more useful than a vent brush for controlling hair of this type.

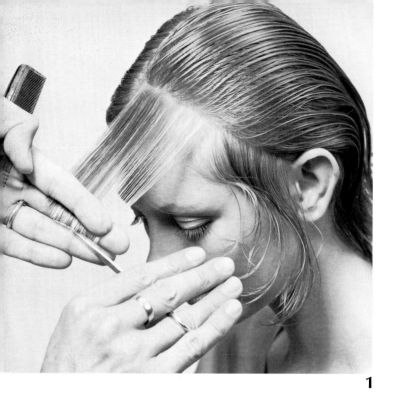

1   2

FIGS. 1 & 2
Take a 1 in. wide section at the front, from the centre parting down to the ear.
Hold the section out and well forward, cut as shown (Figs. 1 & 2).

FIGS. 3 & 4
Take a second section parallel to the first, using the previously-cut line as a
guide (Fig. 3).
Follow through in sections to the centre parting (Fig. 4).

3   4

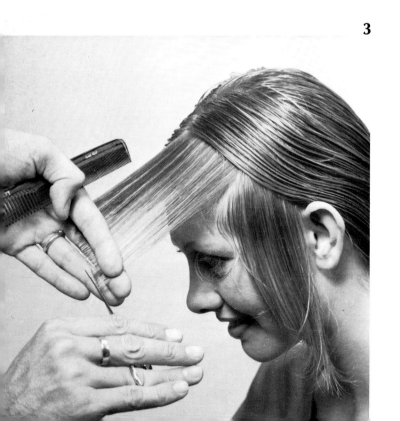

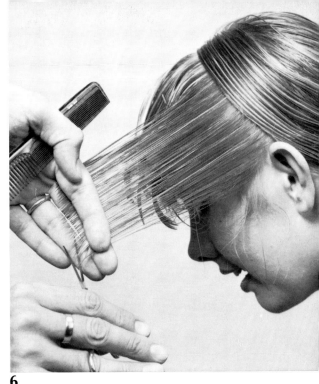

5

6

FIGS. 5 & 6
Continue working back towards the crown (Figs. 5 & 6).

FIGS. 7, 8, 9
Move on to the back area. Take a section parallel to the hairline behind the ear, from the top of the head to the nape (Figs. 7 & 8). Directing the hair forward, cut with previous section (Fig. 6).
Cut length line (Fig. 9).

7

8

9

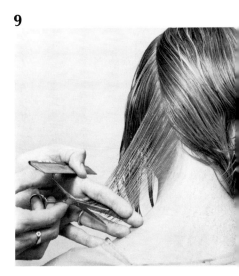

10 **11**   **12**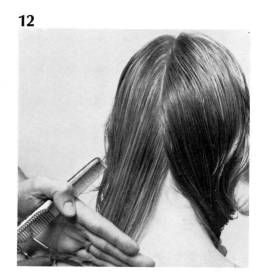

FIGS. 10, 11, 12, 13
Work towards the centre back (Fig. 10).
Continue graduation down the sections towards the nape (Fig. 11).
Cut in length line (Figs. 12 & 13).

FIG. 14
Cross-check length line as you proceed (Fig. 14).

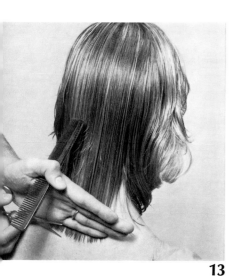 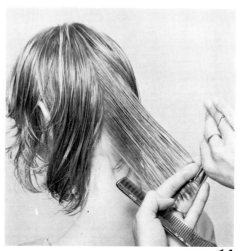 

13 **14** **15**

THE CURLY SHAKE · 158

16 **17**   **18**

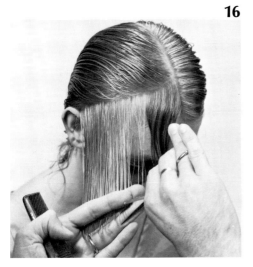 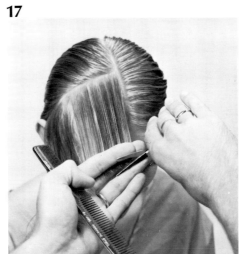 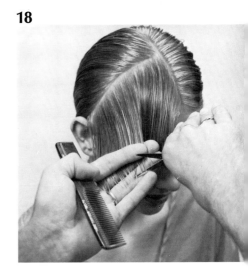

FIGS. 15, 16, 17, 18, 19, 20, 21
Halfway
Section as before, cut as shown (Figs. 15 & 16).
Work back towards the crown (Figs. 17 & 18).
Direct the hair forward at all times (Figs. 19, 20, 21).

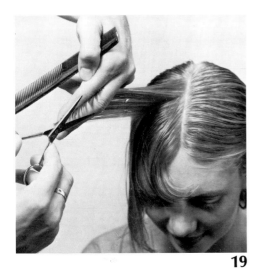  

19 **20**   **21**

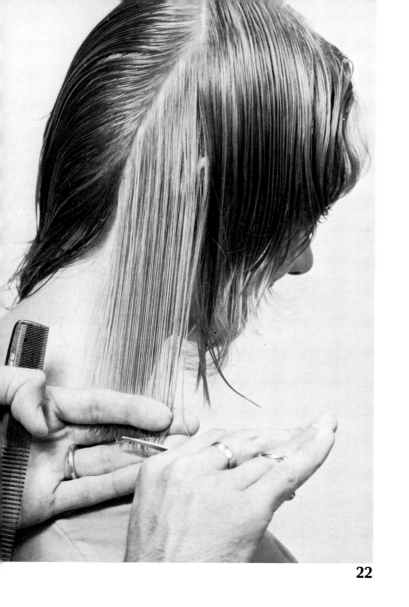

FIGS. 22, 23, 24
Connect the front with the back and
cut the length line (Fig. 22).
Continue cutting in sections towards
centre back, graduating from the
crown to the length line (Figs.
23 & 24).

22

23   24

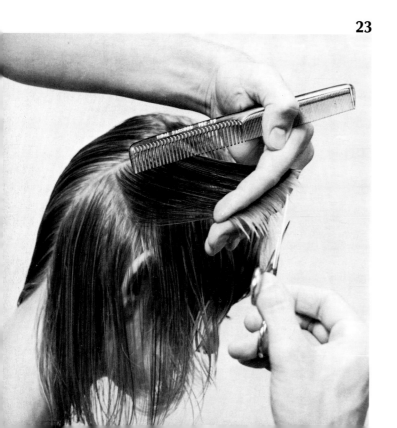

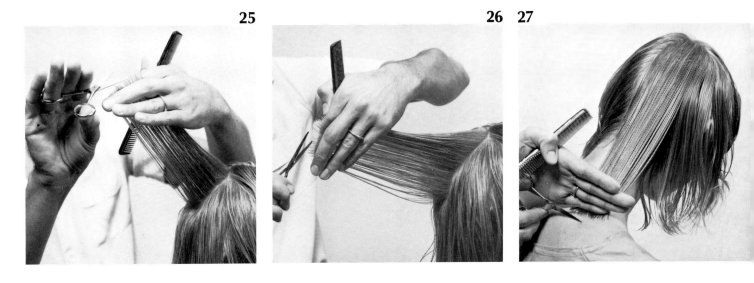

FIGS. 25, 26, 27
When cutting the centre back, do not direct the hair forward as much as before or the back will have too much weight (Figs. 25 & 26).
Comb down, cut in the length line flat against the neck (Fig. 27).

FIG. 28
Cross-check the length line after cutting.

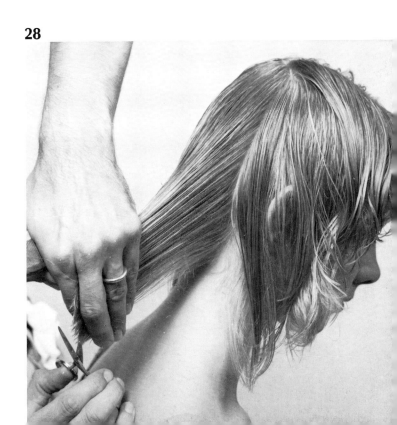

 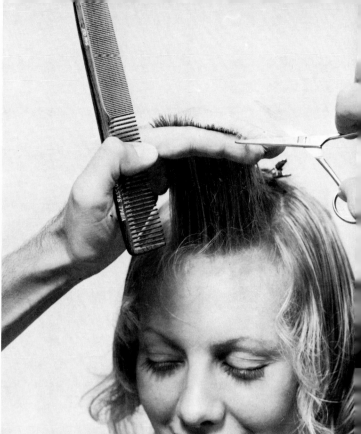

29 30

31 32

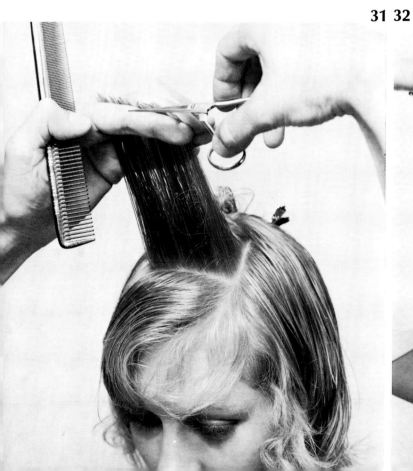 

FIGS. 29, 30, 31, 32
Having cut both sides, check that they match perfectly (Figs. 29, 30, 31).
The hair is then combed into position from the crown and left to dry naturally,
utilizing its natural curl and texture.

33

FIG. 33
The finished result.

GROWING OUT A PERM

Liza's hair has been permed and the perm is now at a growing-out stage.
To help it through this phase, her hair has been shaped through the sides using the 'Firefly' method. The back has been heavily graduated using the same method employed in cutting Fay's naturally curly 'Shake'.

THE LONG SHAKE (1977)

A soft perm creates a mass of all-
over volume and heaviness at the
back; the shorter hair at the sides
and fringe forms naturally into
pretty, face-framing curls.

THE STRAIGHT SHAKE (1977)

The outline is soft, the effect casual,
but the cut is still the essence of this
beautifully layered look, which
features subtle, burnished highlights
to show off the natural texture and
movement of the hair.

KABUKI (1981)

The hair is root permed then cut in graduations from the temple getting longer towards the back. Longer pieces are left over the ears. The hair is then graduated from the temples towards the front to form a peak. The roots are tinted solar-yellow and the rest of the hair coloured volcanic-red.

Root perming gives lift and volume from the base of the hair allowing the top to fall lightly, giving it fullness and density.

VIDAL SASSOON INTERNATIONAL
CREATIVE TEAM

The Senior Partners.
From left to right: Phillip Rogers, Anne Humphreys, Vidal Sassoon and
Christopher Brooker.

This book could never have happened without the inspiration of all the
members of our International Creative Team. Some of their names are
already well known, none more than that of Christopher Brooker, having
appeared in magazines and newspapers all over the world.
Christopher has been the creative talent behind the Vidal Sassoon
organizations for a long time now. As International Creative Director, his
innovative ideas have kept the name Vidal Sassoon in the forefront of
hairdressing and under Christopher's direction, today's creative team
continue to produce their new looks.
Today, Christopher spends much of his time travelling the world, creating
hair shows and well-known Vidal Sassoon seminars for both the trade and
public. On both sides of the Atlantic he is a regular guest on radio and
television shows.
His amazing flair for International beauty trends began as early as 1964

when he left England to tour with me to the Paris Collections. Fine-tuned further through years of hands-on experience with me, Christopher's talents gradually became the trademark for Vidal Sassoon Salons and Academies everywhere.

Earlier in his career, he trained with the original team who were to open the first Vidal Sassoon Salon in New York, he managed the prestigious salons in Europe and eventually became the European Art Director.

Along with Phillip Rogers, Joint Managing Director, and Anne Humphreys, Head of Colour and Technical Research, Christopher has an opportunity to exercise his management and creative skills in one of the most unique international styling operations, ever.

Their success is undoubtedly based on their tremendous sense of team spirit and I hope that this book has enabled you to have a clearer understanding of the fundamental techniques and philosophy that lie behind our organization.

VIDAL SASSOON